GW01465771

Love Those PRECUTS™

Edited by Carolyn S. Vagts

Annie's™

Introduction

Every time I enter a quilt shop, my attention is drawn to those cute precut bundles strategically placed on every counter and end cap. It's eye candy! I know that with the purchase of one of the bundles I can have a small piece of every fabric in the collection. I also know they coordinate perfectly and that many designers create patterns especially for them.

Each of the 12 fabulous quilts in this book was created with one or more types of precuts by our exceptionally talented designers. The projects also include yardage for background, borders and sashing. If you have some of those gorgeous bundles you have been saving, this may be the time to pull them out. Imagine your fabrics in these quilts. If precut inspiration is what you are looking for, here it is.

We have projects for every skill level and projects you can complete in a day or take as long as you like. Go ahead and turn the pages. I'm sure there are a few projects, or maybe all of them, that will call out to you.

For those of you that can only do "controlled" scrappy quilted projects, what better way to start a scrappy project. Any precut could be the beginning of your next project. Make sure to read the tips on how to cut and create your own precut stash. It's a great way to organize your scraps.

Happy quilting!

Carolyn S. Vagts

Key for Precut Icons

Fat Eighths	Charm Pack	Fat Quarters	Layer Cakes	Jelly Rolls

Warm Eyes, **page 13**

Annie's™ *Love Those Precuts* is published by Annie's, 306 East Parr Road, Berne, IN 46711. Printed in USA. Copyright © 2013 Annie's. All rights reserved. This publication may not be reproduced in part or in whole without written permission from the publisher.

RETAIL STORES: If you would like to carry this pattern book or any other Annie's publications, visit AnniesWSL.com

Every effort has been made to ensure that the instructions in this pattern book are complete and accurate. We cannot, however, take responsibility for human error, typographical mistakes or variations in individual work. Please visit AnniesCustomerCare.com to check for pattern updates.

ISBN: 978-1-59217-456-0
1 2 3 4 5 6 7 8 9

Table of Contents

Summer Twist,
page 16

Broken Crackers,
page 27

Celebrate America,
page 42

Macaron Star

Design by Nancy McNally

Use 2½" precut strips and a coordinating background to create a stunning Lone Star. With precuts you're ready to start sewing immediately!

Project Specifications
Skill Level: Advanced
Quilt Size: 60" x 60"

Materials
- 80 (2½" by fabric width) precut strips
- 1 fat quarter coordinating tonal
- 3¼ yards white solid
- 3½ yards backing
- Batting 68" x 68"
- Thread
- Basic sewing tools and supplies

Cutting
1. Cut one 4½" x 22" strip coordinating tonal; subcut four 4½" D squares.

2. Cut two 15½" by fabric width strips white solid; subcut four 15½" A squares.

3. Cut one 21½" by fabric width strip white solid; subcut one 21½" square. Cut the square on both diagonals to make four B triangles.

4. Cut eight 2½" by fabric width strips white solid for strip sets.

5. Cut six 4½" by fabric width C strips white solid.

Completing the Star Points
1. Sort 2½" precut strips into five groups of like colors: teal, white, purple, red and green.

2. Select one each teal and white and three purple strips. Join strips lengthwise in order for Strip Set 1 and staggered 2½" as shown in Figure 1; press seams in one direction. Repeat for Strip Sets 2–5 referring again to Figure 1; press seams in opposite directions between strip sets. Label strip sets.

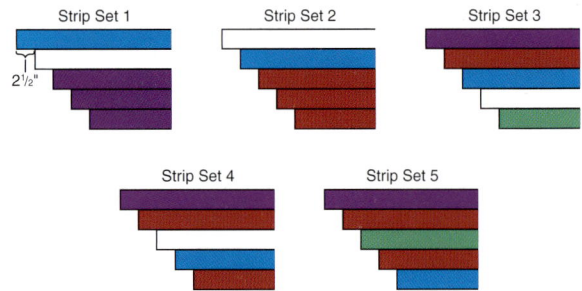

Figure 1

3. Make at least two extra strip sets any combination and label for first border and binding.

4. Place 45-degree line on ruler at bottom edge of Strip Set 1 and trim strip set edge at a 45-degree angle, cutting off staggered ends as shown in Figure 2.

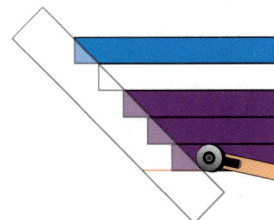

Figure 2

5. Cut Strip Set 1 into 2½"-wide strips referring to Figure 3.

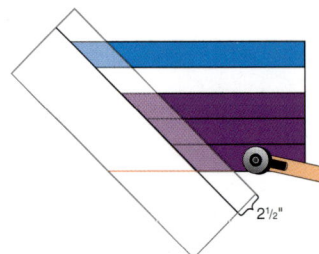

Figure 3

6. Repeat steps 4 and 5 with all strip sets. Label and arrange pieced strips in strip sets. Set aside strips cut from strip sets made for border one.

7. Select and arrange one strip from each strip set as shown in Figure 4.

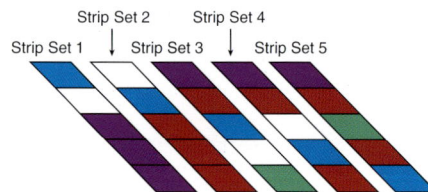

Figure 4

Constructing a Perfect Y Seam

Some designs require set-in pieces where three seams coming together make a Y shape (Figure A). This is accomplished with a set-in or Y seam.

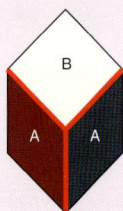

Figure A

Stopping stitching at seam intersections, pressing and stitching from an inside point to an outside point are all equally important to a perfect Y seam.

Refer to the following instructions to make quilts with perfect set-in pieces.

1. Using a large needle or small paper punch, make a hole in the templates at the seam intersections marked with dots on patterns as shown in Figure B. Transfer seam intersection dots by marking the fabric through the template holes.

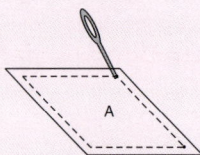

Figure B

2. Stitch the first leg of a Y seam by selecting two diamond-shaped pieces (A) and joining; start stitching at the marked dot and end at the end of the seam as shown in Figure C. Backstitch at the beginning of the seam to lock the stitches.

Figure C

3. Press this seam open referring to Figure D. Trim seam ends even with A pieces, again referring to Figure D.

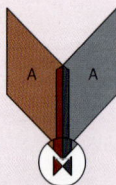

Figure D

4. Set in a square piece (B) for the second leg of the Y seam, starting stitching at the marked dots on the joined A unit and backstitching to lock seams as shown in Figure E.

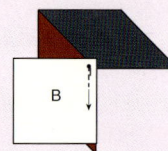

Figure E

5. Stitch to the end of the seam as usual as shown in Figure F. Press seams away from B, again referring to Figure F.

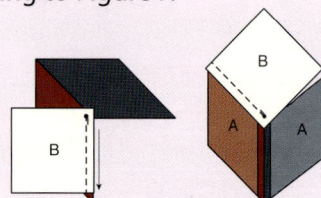

Figure F

6. To complete the final Y seam, stitch the second side of B to the A unit in the same manner, starting at the dot and stitching to the outside edge as shown in Figure G and press seam away from B as shown in Figure H.

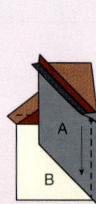

Figure G

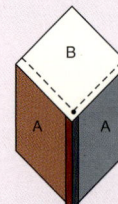

Figure H

8. Join strips in order arranged, matching seams, to make a Lone Star point as shown in Figure 5. Select, arrange and join strips in this manner to make eight star points.

Star Point
Make 8

Figure 5

Completing the Lone Star

1. Mark a placement dot on one corner of each A square and the 45-degree angle of each B triangle as shown in Figure 6. Set aside.

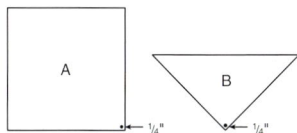

A   B

¼"   ¼"

Figure 6

2. Join star points in pairs as shown in Figure 7, beginning stitching ¼" from edge; backstitch to secure. Press seams all in same direction.

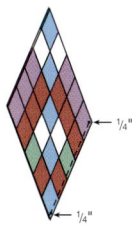

¼"

¼"

Figure 7

3. Referring to Constructing a Perfect Y Seam and Figure 8, insert an A square between the star points of one pair; press seams toward the star points. Repeat to make four A-star point units.

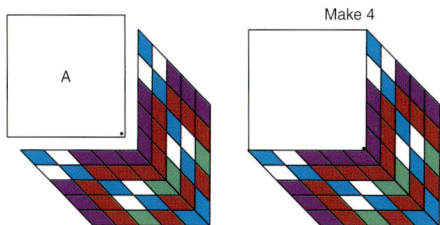

A   Make 4

Figure 8

4. Join two A-star point units together referring to Figure 7 and step 2.

5. Insert a B triangle between the A-star point units as shown in Figure 9 using a Y seam; press seams toward the star points. Repeat to make two halves of the Lone Star, again referring to Figure 9.

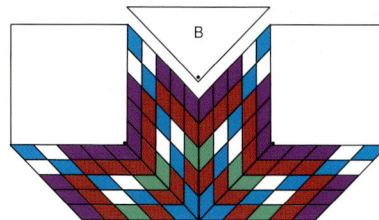

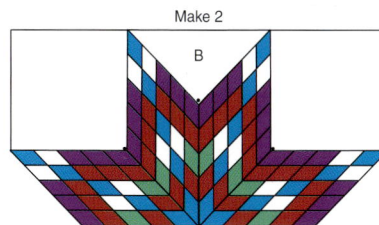

B

Make 2
B

Figure 9

6. Referring to Figure 10, join the halves of the Lone Star along the star point edges beginning and ending stitching ¼" from the ends of the seam; backstitch to secure both ends. Press seams in same direction as the rest of the star point seams.

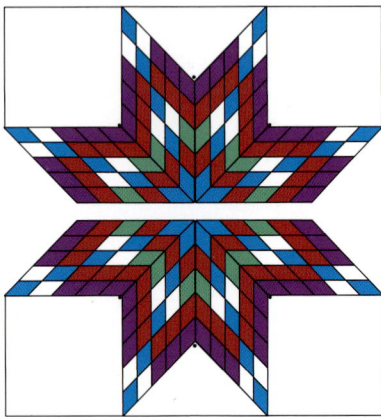

Figure 10

7. Insert B triangles between the star points as shown in Figure 11 using Y seams; press seams toward star points.

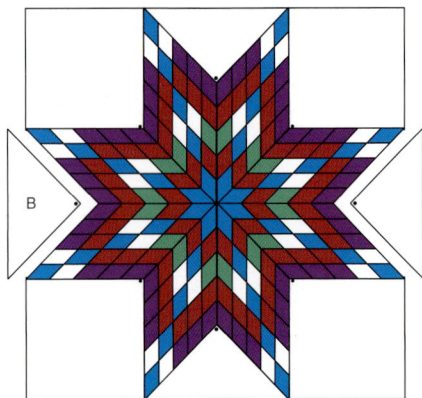

Figure 11

Completing the Quilt

1. Stitch remaining strips from strip sets into two sets of four strips each for two side borders.

2. Center and stitch a pieced side border to a quilt side; press seam away from quilt. Trim pieced side border even with quilt top and bottom. Repeat on opposite side.

3. Repeat steps 1 and 2 to make and join pieced top and bottom borders to the quilt referring to the Assembly Diagram.

4. Stitch C strips together on short ends to make one long strip; press seams in one direction. Cut long strip into four 4½" x 52½" C border strips.

5. Stitch a C border strip to both sides of the quilt referring to the Assembly Diagram.

6. Join a D square to both ends of a C border strip. Repeat to make two C-D border strips.

7. Stitch a C-D border strip to the top and bottom of the quilt referring to the Assembly Diagram.

8. Stitch any 2½"-wide precut strips left over from completing the strip sets together with angled seams to make one long strip for binding at least 250" long; press seams in one direction.

9. Layer, quilt as desired and bind. ■

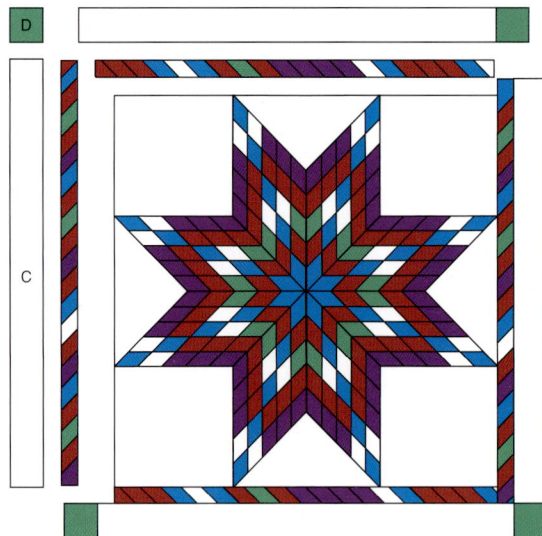

Macaron Star
Assembly Diagram 60" x 60"

Apple of My Eye

Design by Wendy Sheppard

Fat quarters, or a collection of 10" squares, could easily make this quilt.

Project Specifications

Skill Level: Confident Beginner
Quilt Size: 50" x 50"
Block Size: 2" x 2"
Number of Blocks: 56

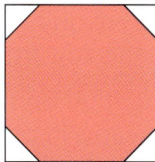

Snowball Block
2" x 2" Block
Make 56

Materials

- 5 fat quarter bright pastel prints
- 5 fat quarter coordinating pastel tonals
- ½ yard pastel floral print
- 1¼ yards apple print
- 1⅜ yards white solid
- 3¼ yards backing
- Batting 58" x 58"
- Thread
- Basic sewing tools and supplies

Cutting

1. Cut a total of 49 (3½") E squares from the bright pastel print fat quarters.

2. Cut a total of 64 (2½") B squares from the coordinating pastel tonal fat quarters.

3. Cut five 2½" by fabric width H/I strips pastel floral print.

4. Cut five 3½" by fabric width L/M strips apple print.

5. Cut six 2¼ by fabric width strips apple print for binding.

6. Cut nine 2½" by fabric width strips white solid; subcut 104 (2½" x 3½") C rectangles.

7. Cut six 1" by fabric width strips white solid; subcut 224 (1") A squares.

8. Cut nine 1¼" by fabric width strips; subcut two each 1¼" x 37½" G and 1¼" x 39" F border strips. Set aside remaining strips for J and K borders.

Completing the Blocks

1. Draw diagonal lines on wrong side of all A squares.

2. Position A in one corner of B referring to Figure 1 and stitch on marked line. Trim seam to ¼" and press A away from B. Repeat on all four corners of B.

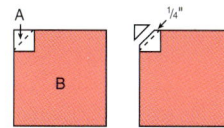

Figure 1

3. Repeat step 2 to make 64 Snowball blocks.

Completing the Quilt Center

1. Select, arrange as desired and join seven Snowball blocks and eight C rectangles alternately as shown in Figure 2 to make Row 1. Press seams toward C. Make a total of eight rows. **Note:** *The designer chose to make two each pink, yellow and blue rows and two red and green rows as seen in the Assembly Diagram.*

Row 1
Make 8

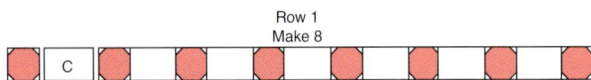

Figure 2

2. Select, arrange as desired and join seven assorted E squares and eight D rectangles alternately referring to Figure 3 to make Row 2. Press seams toward C. Make a total of seven rows.

Row 2
Make 7

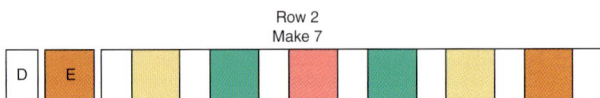

Figure 3

3. Join rows along length alternately beginning and ending with Row 1 and referring to the Assembly Diagram. Press seams in one direction. **Note:** *The Assembly Diagram shows the designer's row placement. If you do not arrange Row 2 like the designer your quilt center will look different.*

Completing the Quilt

1. Stitch G strips to the quilt center sides; press seam toward G. Stitch F strips to quilt center top and bottom; press seams toward F.

2. Stitch H/I strips together on short ends to make one long strip; press seams in one direction. Cut strip into two each 2½" x 39" H side borders and 2½" x 43" I top/bottom borders.

3. Stitch H to both sides of quilt top and I to top and bottom; press seams toward H and I.

4. Stitch the J/K strips together on short ends to make one long strip; press seams in one direction. Cut strip into two each 1¼" x 43" J side borders and 1¼" x 44½" K top/bottom borders.

5. Stitch J to both sides of quilt top and K to top and bottom; press seams toward J and K.

6. Stitch L/M strips together on short ends to make one long strip; press seams in one direction. Cut strip into two each 3½" x 44½" L side borders and 3½" x 50½" M top/bottom borders.

7. Stitch L to both sides of quilt top and M to top and bottom; press seams toward L and M.

8. Layer, quilt as desired and bind. ■

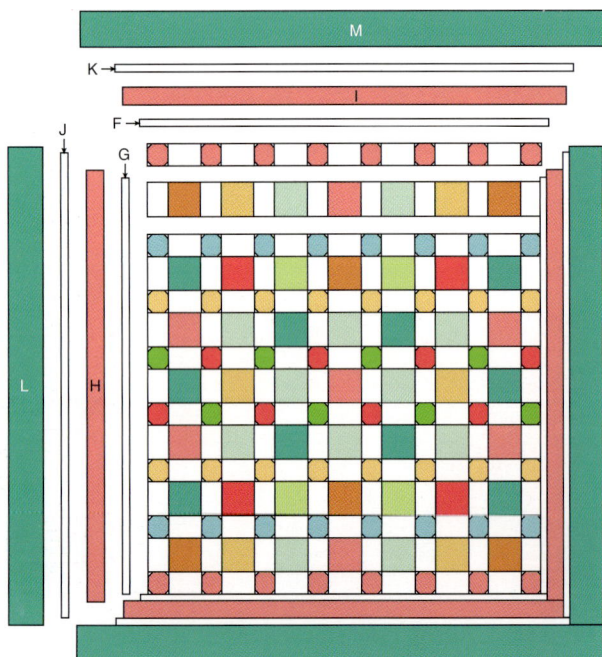

Apple of My Eye
Assembly Diagram 50" x 50"

Tips

Even though precuts are supposed to be standard sizes, they can vary in size between manufacturers. Measure precuts before subcutting or stitching to verify their size. If the edges are pinked, measure between the outside points of the pinking.

With patterns designed specifically for precuts and their increased popularity, some quilt shops are now cutting their own precuts, especially fat quarters. You might find them willing to cut you a fat quarter instead of a ¼ yard. Why not ask?

Warm Eyes

Design by Bev Remillard

A fun collection of fat quarters, or 5" or 10" squares, some coordinating yardage and the appliqué technique of your choice is all you need to create this beauty.

Project Specifications

Skill Level: Intermediate
Quilt Size: 62" x 62"
Block Size: 11" x 11"
Number of Blocks: 13

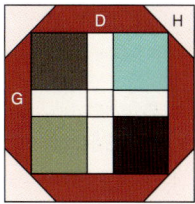

Medium Sashing Block
11" x 11" Block
Make 9

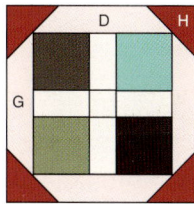

Light Sashing Block
11" x 11" Block
Make 4

Materials

- 1 coordinating fat quarter dark solid
- 3 coordinating fat quarters light solid
- 20 coordinating fat quarter prints
- 1⅜ yards white solid
- 4 yards backing
- Batting 70" x 70"
- Thread
- ½ yard paper-backed fusible web (optional)
- 13 (1½" diameter) coordinating buttons
- Basic sewing tools and supplies

Cutting

1. Prepare Petal appliqué templates for use with your favorite appliqué technique. Cut 16 dark petals and 36 light petals from dark and light coordinating solid fat quarters. Set aside. *Note: Appliqué patterns provided are for fusible appliqué. Adjust the patterns for your favorite appliqué technique.*

2. Sort fat quarter prints into three groups: Group 1, eight lightest prints; Group 2, six medium prints; Group 3, six darkest prints. *Note: To have an even scrappier look, use 5" or 10" precut squares to cut the dark print A and C squares, medium print I squares and light print H squares as listed below. Cut strips*

for D, E, F, G, L/M and N/O from fat quarter groups as listed below.

3. Cut two 4" x 22" strips from each Group 3 fat quarter; subcut a total of 52 (4") A squares.

4. Cut at least 18 (2" x 22") strips from remainder of Group 1 fat quarter prints; subcut a total of 13 (2") C squares. Set aside remainder of strips for N/O second border.

5. Cut one 3½" x 22" strip from each of the Group 1 fat quarters; subcut a total of 36 (3½") H squares. Draw a diagonal line on wrong side of each square.

6. Cut two 1½" x 22" strips from each Group 1 fat quarter; subcut into a total of eight each 1½" x 9" D strips and 1½" x 13" E strips.

7. Cut at least 13 (3½" x 22") P/Q strips from remainder of Group 1 fat quarters for third border.

8. Cut one 3½" x 22" strip from each of the Group 2 fat quarters; subcut a total of 16 (3½") I squares. Draw a diagonal line on wrong side of each square.

Subcutting Precuts

Just because you have the perfect fabric in a precut size that is not listed in the materials list, don't be discouraged! Take advantage of the precuts you have. Treat it as yardage and subcut it into the sizes you need.

Do you need squares, triangles, sashing strips? They could all be cut from a 10" square.

For example, cut 10" squares in half for 5" x 10" rectangles. Cut in half again for four 5" squares. Finally, cut the 5" squares into 2½" squares. Or, cut four 2½" x 10" sashing strips.

You can subcut up to six layers of fabric with control using 10" squares.

9. Cut five 1½" x 22" strips from each Group 2 fat quarter; subcut a total of 18 each 1½" x 9" F strips and 1½" x 13" G strips.

10. Cut at least 11 (1½" x 22") L/M strips from remainder of Group 2 fat quarters for first border.

11. Cut three 4" by fabric width strips white solid; subcut 52 (2" x 4") B rectangles.

12. Cut one 18½" by fabric width strip white solid; subcut into two 18½" squares. Cut each square on both diagonals to cut four K triangles.

13. Cut one 10" by fabric width strip white solid; subcut two 10" squares. Cut each square on one diagonal to cut four J triangles.

Completing the Blocks

1. Join four each A squares and B rectangles and one C square into a Nine-Patch unit as shown in Figure 1. Press seams toward A and C. Repeat to make 13 units.

Figure 1

2. Stitch a D strip to top and bottom of a Nine-Patch unit and an E strip to opposite sides referring to Figure 2; press seams toward D and E.

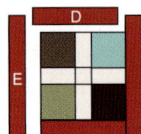

Figure 2

3. Select four I squares. Position an I square on one corner of the Nine-Patch unit and stitch along the marked diagonal line as shown in Figure 3. Trim seam to ¼" and press I away from the unit. Repeat on all 4 corners referring again to Figure 3.

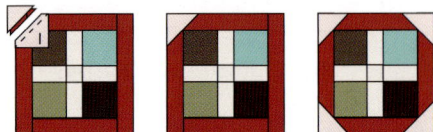

Figure 3

4. Repeat steps 1–3 to make four Light Sashing blocks.

5. Refer to block diagram and repeat steps 1–3 with nine Nine-Patch units, F and G strips and H squares to make nine Medium Sashing blocks.

6. Fold and crease a Light Sashing block on both diagonals. Position and apply dark petals at block center on diagonals using your favorite appliqué technique and referring to the block diagrams.

7. Appliqué dark petals to Light Sashing blocks and light petals to Medium Sashing blocks to complete 13 blocks.

Completing the Quilt Center

1. Stitch K triangles to sides of a completed Medium Sashing block (Figure 4); press seams toward K.

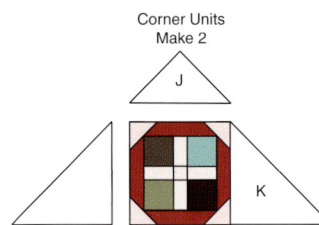

Corner Units
Make 2

Figure 4

2. Stitch J triangle to top of a Medium Sashing block referring again to Figure 4; press seam toward J.

3. Repeat steps 1 and 2 to make two corner units.

4. Stitch two Medium Sashing blocks, one Light Sashing block and two K triangles together, as shown in Figure 5, to make Row 1. Repeat to make two rows. Trim setting triangles even with blocks.

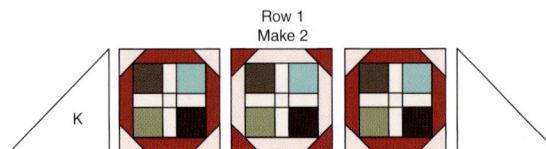

Row 1
Make 2

Figure 5

Tip

Precut bundles were introduced to show all the variations within a fabric collection. If you have trouble with color coordination, precuts may be the answer. Not only is the cutting process shortened, but fabric coordination is no longer guesswork.

5. Stitch three Medium Sashing blocks, two Light Sashing blocks and two J triangles together, as shown in Figure 6, to make a center row.

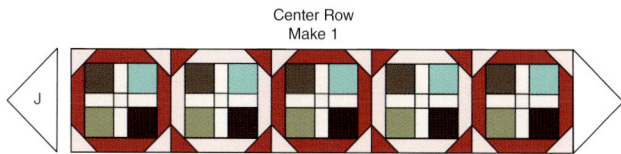

Center Row
Make 1

Figure 6

6. Join two each corner units and Row 1 and center row diagonally referring to Assembly Diagram to complete pieced quilt center.

Completing the Quilt

1. Stitch 1½" x 22" L/M Group 2 strips together on short ends to make one long strip; press seams in one direction. Cut L/M strip into two each 1½" x 51¼" L and 1½" x 53¼" M strips for first border.

2. Stitch L to top and bottom of quilt center and M to both sides referring to Assembly Diagram.

3. Stitch 2" x 22" N/O Group 3 strips together on short ends to make one long strip; press seams in one direction. Cut N/O strip into two each 1½" x 53¼" N and 1½" x 56¼" O strips for first border.

4. Stitch N to top and bottom of quilt center and O to both sides referring to Assembly Diagram.

5. Stitch 3½" x 22" P/Q Group 1 strips together on short ends to make one long strip; press seams in one direction. Cut P/Q strip into two each 1½" x 56¼" P and 1½" x 62¼" Q strips for first border.

6. Stitch P to top and bottom of quilt center and Q to both sides referring to Assembly Diagram.

7. Layer, quilt as desired and bind. ***Note:*** *The designer cut 2½" x 22" strips from remaining fat quarters for binding. If you prefer a solid binding, you will need to purchase ⅞ yard of coordinating fabric.* ■

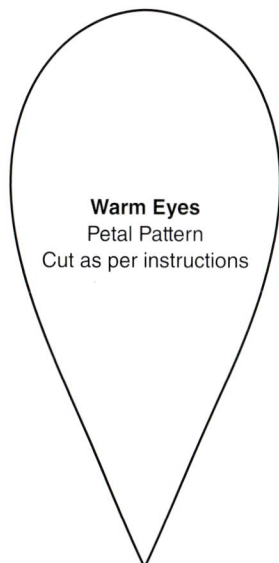

Warm Eyes
Petal Pattern
Cut as per instructions

Tip

If the edges of your precuts are pinked, don't trim them straight. You will change their overall size. Use the outer points of the pinked edge as the fabric edge when aligning edges for stitching or subcutting.

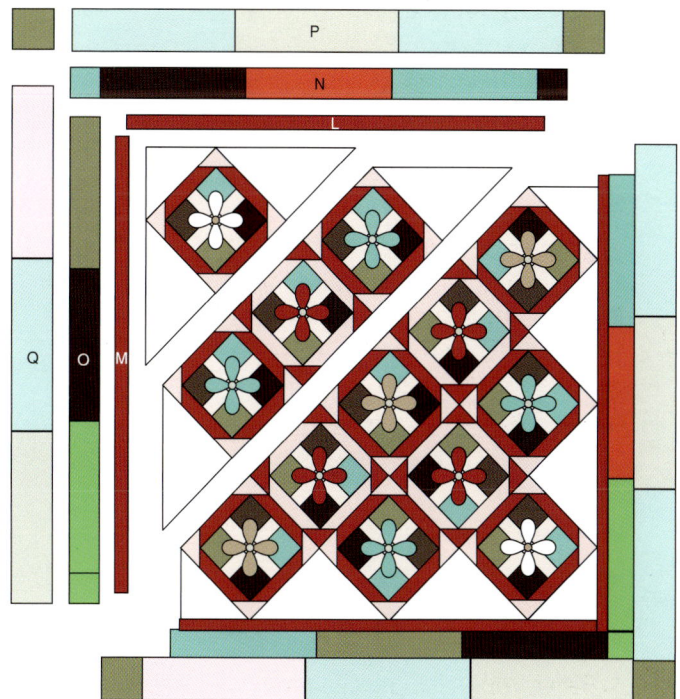

Warm Eyes
Assembly Diagram 62" x 62"

Summer Twist

Design by Tricia Lynn Maloney

Quilted by Karen Shields of Karen's Quilting Studio

A large, simple graphic quilt block makes short work of this breezy bed quilt.

Project Specifications
Skill Level: Intermediate
Quilt Size: 67½" x 90"
Block Size: 22½" x 22½"
Number of Blocks: 12

Twist Block
22½" x 22½" Block
Make 12

Materials
- 96 assorted 5" precut A squares
- ⅞ yard coordinating solid
- 3⅞ yards white solid
- 6 yards backing
- Batting 76" x 98"
- Thread
- Basic sewing tools and supplies

Cutting
1. Cut eight 2¼" by fabric width strips coordinating solid for binding.

2. Cut eight 5" by fabric width strips white solid; subcut into 60 (5") B squares.

3. Cut six 14" by fabric width strips white solid; subcut into 48 (5" x 14") C rectangles.

Tip

Resist the notion to wash precuts! Washing might cause the fabric to fray, ravel or shrink. Which means your 10" precut square probably won't be 10" square.

Completing the Blocks
1. Stitch a 5" precut A square between two B squares. Repeat to make two B-A-B rows.

2. Stitch a B square between two A charm squares.

3. Stitch the B-A-B row between two A-B-A rows referring to Figure 1 to make a Nine-Patch unit.

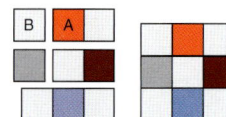

Figure 1

4. Stitch an A square to the end of a C rectangle (Figure 2). Repeat to make four C-A strips.

Make 4

Figure 2

5. Position and stitch a C-A strip on the top of the Nine-Patch unit using a partial seam with the C end extending beyond the left side as shown in Figure 3. Press seam away from the Nine-Patch unit.

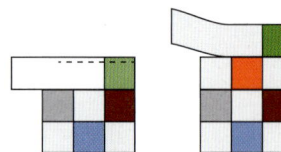

Figure 3

6. Stitch C-A strips to right side and then the bottom of the Nine-Patch unit referring to Figure 4. Always match A to a B square on the Nine-Patch unit and press seams away from the unit.

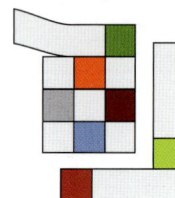

Figure 4

Making Precuts From Your Stash

Every quilter has scraps. And we have all suffered from the decision involved in how to store and use them. Here's an idea. Why not use that mountain of scraps to create your own precuts.

Manufacturers sell precuts in standard sizes most frequently used in all types of quilts. Follow their lead and cut your scraps into 2½"-wide strips and 5" and 10" squares.

- Begin by sorting your scraps by size. Press scraps flat.
- Make a straight cut as close to the straight grain of the fabric as possible along the longest edge of the scrap.
- Position your ruler along this edge at the width you want and make your second cut.
- Cut strips 2½" wide the minimum length you choose. For example, if you like scrappy bindings you may decide you would prefer strips 10" or longer. Shorter-length strips can be used later to subcut 2½" or smaller squares.
- Cut 5" and 10" squares from larger scraps by first cutting strips and then subcutting into squares.
- Trim similarly sized scraps into 5" or 10" squares paying attention to the straight of grain.
- Create fat eighths (9" x 21") and fat quarters (18" x 21") from leftover ⅛, ¼ and ½ yard pieces.

Sort and store your precut stash by size and color family to make them easier to find and use. You will be surprised at how fast that stash disappears.

7. Stitch a C-A strip to the left side of the Nine-Patch unit, keeping the top C-A strip free of stitching (Figure 5). Press seam away from the Nine-Patch unit.

Figure 5

8. Complete the top strip seam as shown in Figure 6; press seam away from the Nine-Patch unit.

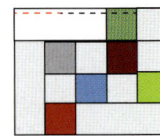

Figure 6

9. Repeat steps 1–8 to make 12 Twist blocks.

Completing the Quilt

1. Arrange and stitch Twist blocks in four rows of three blocks each referring to the Assembly Diagram.

2. Layer, quilt as desired and bind. ■

Summer Twist
Assembly Diagram 67½" x 90"

Hanging Lanterns

Design by Bev Getschel

Turn a stack of fat eighths into a dramatic wall hanging that will be the focal point of any room where it is displayed.

Project Specifications
Skill Level: Intermediate
Quilt Size: 48" x 60"

Project Note
Whether selecting your fabrics from a collection as the designer did or just choosing coordinating prints, be sure to include some white or cream to be used in the lantern centers and quilt border.

Materials
- 20 fat eighths assorted oriental prints
- ⅝ yard black print
- ¾ yard aqua tonal
- 1⅝ yards black solid
- 3⅛ yards backing
- Batting 56" x 68"
- Thread
- Gold machine embroidery thread
- Freezer paper
- 3" x 19" paper-backed fusible web (optional)
- Basic sewing tools and supplies

Cutting
1. Set aside one white fat eighth for lantern centers.

2. Prepare templates for 7½", 6½", 5½", 4½" and 3½" long wedges from wedge pattern provided.

3. Referring to Figures 1–3 for fat eighth cutting diagrams, cut a total of 15 (7½"), 36 (6½"), 28 (5½"), 28 (4½") and 33 (3½") wedges from 14 assorted fat eighth prints.

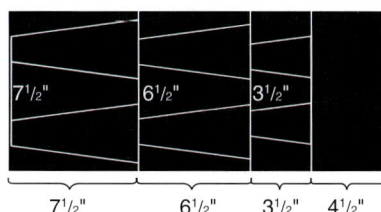

Figure 1

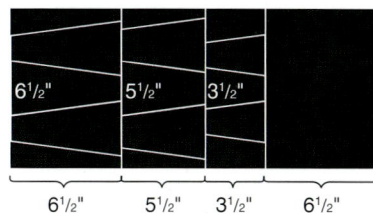

Figure 2

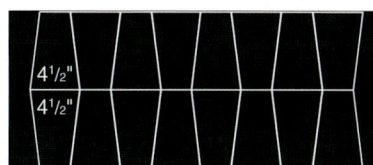

Figure 3

4. Cut five 2½" by fabric width C/D strips black print.

5. Cut six 2¼" by fabric width strips aqua tonal for binding.

6. Cut one 3" by fabric width strip aqua tonal; subcut one 3" x 19" strip. Apply paper-backed fusible web to wrong side of strip following manufacturer's instructions. Cut the fused strip into four ⅝" x 19" A strips.

7. Cut seven 3½" circles from white fat eighth for your favorite appliqué technique. ***Note:*** *Pattern provided without seam allowances for fusible appliqué.*

8. Cut a total of 178 (4½") wedges from remaining fat eighths, black print and aqua for pieced borders referring again to Figure 3.

9. Cut one 36½" x 48½" B background black solid.

Completing the Lantern Appliqués

1. Referring to Figure 4, join two each 6½" and 5½" wedges and three each 4½" and 3½" wedges to make the top half of a Large Lantern appliqué; press seams to one side.

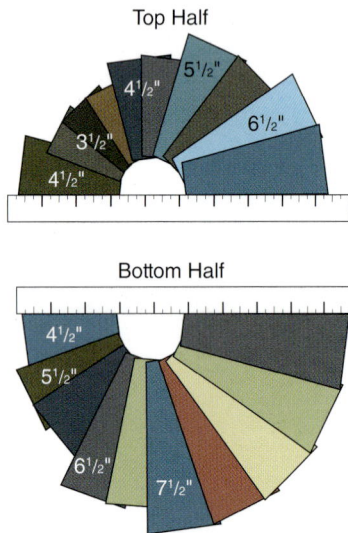

Figure 4

2. Join five 7½", two each 6½" and 5½" and one 4½" wedges to make bottom half of Large Lantern appliqué referring again to Figure 4; press seams to one side.

3. Stitch lantern halves together to create Large Lanterns. Apply 3½" white circle over center opening using your favorite appliqué technique and machine-stitch a decorative stitch around the circle circumference. *Note: Since this circle is being appliquéd over an open area, be careful using a fusible appliqué technique. Cut any fusible web out of the center of the circle before application.*

4. Cut and fold a 14" square of freezer paper into fourths. Use the quarter circle pattern provided to cut a 12½" circle from the folded freezer paper.

5. Unfold and center the shiny side of the freezer paper circle pattern on a Large Lantern; press in place with a dry iron to secure. Trim the lantern even with the circle pattern edges referring to Figure 5.

6. Repeat steps 1–5 to make three Large Lanterns.

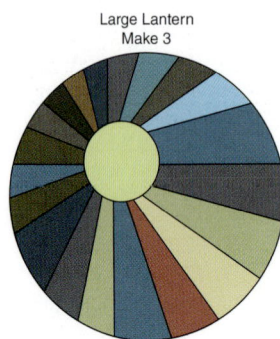

Large Lantern
Make 3

Figure 5

7. Use six each 6½" and 3½" wedges, four each 5½" and 4½" wedges, one 3½" white circle and the 10½" circle pattern to make a Small Lantern appliqué referring to steps 1–5 above.

8. Prepare completed lanterns for favorite appliqué method. *Note: If using turned edge appliqué, you may want to staystitch the lantern edges ⅛" to ¼" in from the outer edges to keep seams from pulling apart during handling.*

Completing the Appliqué Center

1. Draw three lines 9⅛" apart along the length of B background (Figure 6).

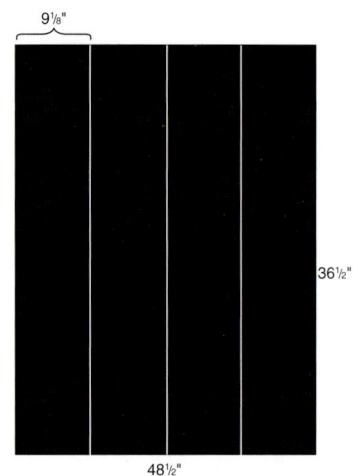

Figure 6

2. Center and arrange Large Lanterns over center line and two Small Lanterns on left and right lines referring to Assembly Diagram and photo.

3. Center A strips over lines between the lanterns referring to the Assembly Diagram. Trim strips so that they will be caught in the top border seam and tucked under lantern edges. Fuse in place following fusible web manufacturer's instructions.

4. Appliqué lanterns to B background using your favorite appliqué method. Machine-stitch a decorative stitch using gold thread around the outer edges of the lanterns and along both sides of the A strips.

Completing the Quilt

1. Stitch C/D strips together on short ends to make one long strip; press seams in one direction. Cut strip into two each 2½" x 40½" C border strips and 2½" x 48½" D borders.

2. Stitch C to top and bottom of B and D to both sides; press seams toward borders.

3. Join 56 (4½") wedges together matching wide ends to narrow ends and varying color placement to make a pieced top border. Repeat to make a pieced bottom border.

4. Join 43 (4½") wedges together matching wide ends to narrow ends and varying color placement to make a pieced side border. Repeat to make two pieced side borders.

5. Stitch pieced side borders to both sides of quilt; press seams toward C. Stitch top and bottom pieced borders to quilt; press seams toward D.

6. Layer, quilt as desired and bind. ■

Precut Common Names

Although some precut sizes are now commonly referred to by the names they were first introduced by, those names were trademarks of the original manufacturer. For example, all quilters are in the habit of referring to 2½" by fabric width strip bundles as Jelly Rolls™, the trademark name of Moda fabrics.

This is why the projects in this book list precuts by size, not name, in the materials lists. When you are shopping for precuts, you will notice that each manufacturer who offers precut bundles will refer to them by their own names. Be sure to purchase your precuts by size.

Here are just a few of the manufacturer names you will see for the sizes used in this book.

2½" by fabric width strip bundles
Moda	Jelly Rolls
Hoffman	Bali Pops
Timeless Treasures	Treat Strips
Riley Blake Designs	RoliePolies

5" square bundles
Moda	Charms
Hoffman	Snaps
Timeless Treasures	Treat Minis
Riley Blake Designs	Stackers

10" square bundles
Moda	Layer Cakes
Hoffman	Crackers
Timeless Treasures	Treat Squares
Riley Blake Designs	Stackers

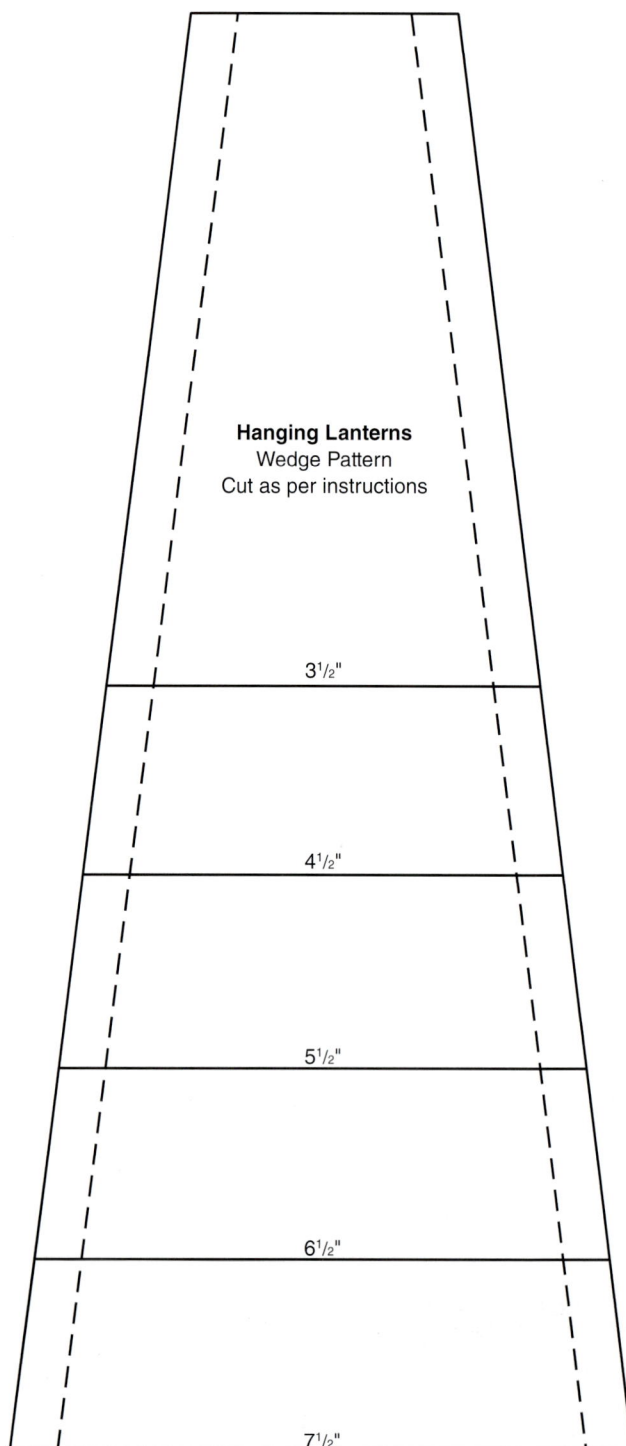

Hanging Lanterns
Wedge Pattern
Cut as per instructions

3½"

4½"

5½"

6½"

7½"

Tip

Test for running or bleeding color by carefully steaming a precut between muslin pieces.

On completing your quilt, launder it with a Shout Color Catcher (or several!) to catch any dyes during washing.

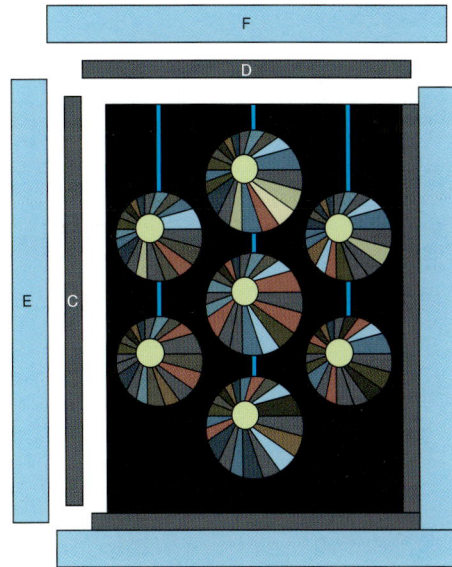

Hanging Lanterns
Assembly Diagram 48" x 60"

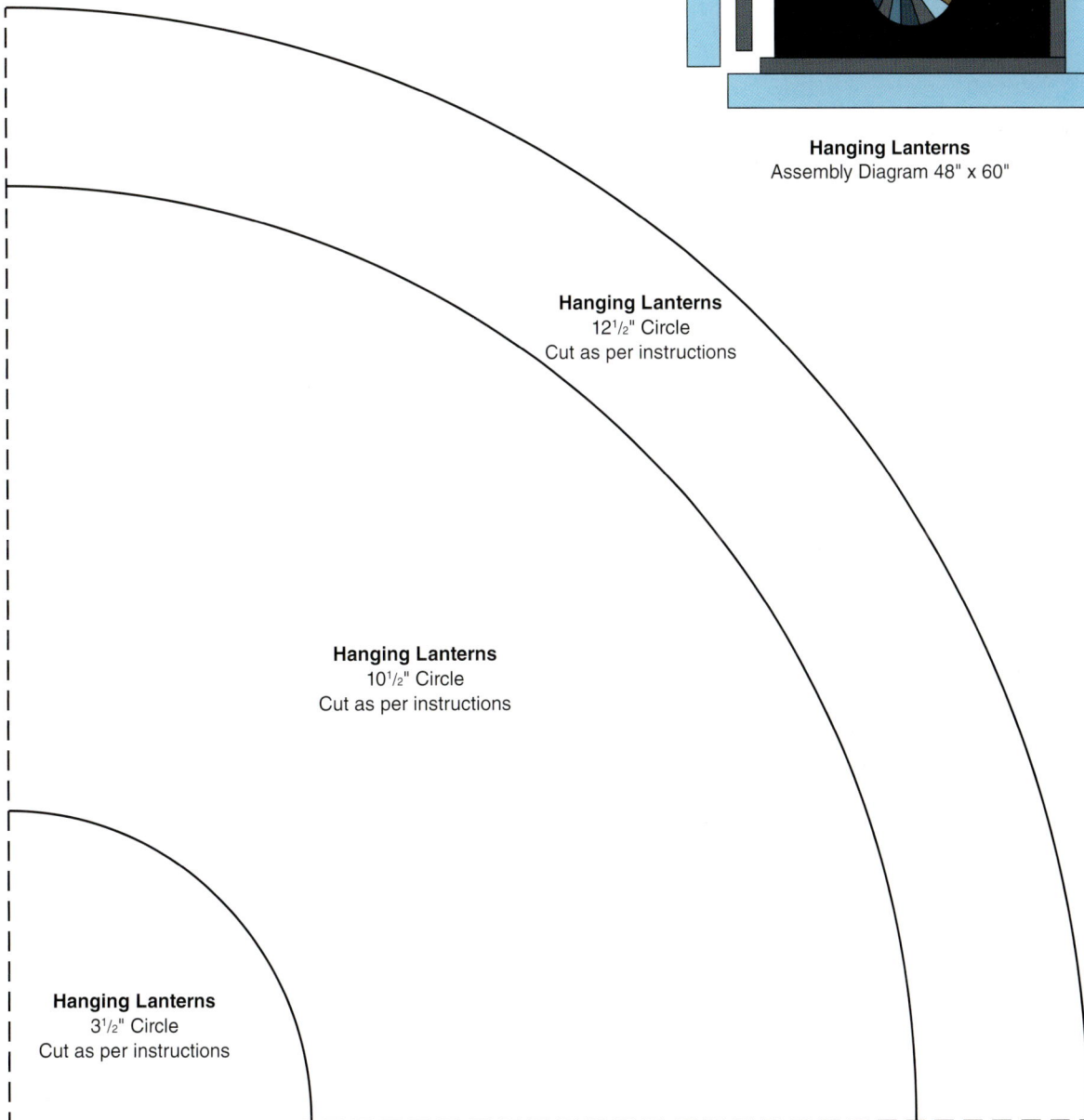

Hanging Lanterns
12¹/₂" Circle
Cut as per instructions

Hanging Lanterns
10¹/₂" Circle
Cut as per instructions

Hanging Lanterns
3¹/₂" Circle
Cut as per instructions

Pretty in Pink

Design by Missy Shepler

This flexible design, using precut 2½" strips stretched across a bright white background, can easily be completed in a weekend.

Project Specifications
Skill Level: Confident Beginner
Quilt Size: 60" x 74"

Project Note
Don't be afraid of all the pieces in this quilt. The trick to making the construction easy is to label the pieces as you cut and keep like sizes together. As rows are completed, label them as well.

Materials
- 28 (2½" by fabric width) precut strips bright pink prints
- 2⅞ yards white solid
- 4¼ yards backing
- Batting 68" x 82"
- Thread
- Even Feed or Walking sewing machine foot
- Basic sewing tools and supplies

Cutting
1. From the 2½" by fabric width precut strips, cut:

5—2½" x 32½" B strips	2—2½" x 30½" C strips
1—2½" x 28½" D strip	2—2½" x 16½" E strips
1—2½" x 14½" F strip	3—2½" x 12½" G strips
2—2½" x 10½" H strips	1—2½" x 8½" I strip
7—2½" x 6½" J strips	1—2½" x 4½" K strip

2. Cut a total of 128 (2½") A squares from the precut strips. *Note: Cut the squares from a variety of the strips to make a more colorful quilt.*

3. Trim the remainder of the precut strips to 2¼" wide for binding.

4. Cut 12 (2½" by fabric width) strips white solid; subcut eight 2½" x 40½" L1 strips and eight 2½" x 20½" L2 strips.

5. With remainder of white solid lengthwise, cut one each:

10½" x 60½" Row 3	6½" x 60½" Row 5
12½" x 60½" Row 7	8½" x 60½" Row 9

Completing the Rows
1. Select, arrange and join nine A squares and one each D and F strip into Row 2 referring to Figure 1 for arrangement; press seams in one direction.

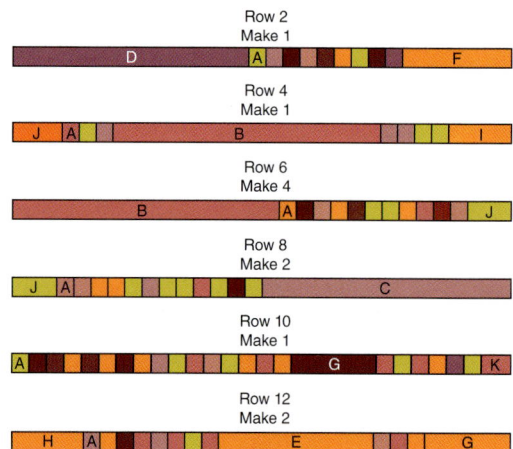

Figure 1

2. Select number of pieces as noted here for each row. Then arrange and join the pieces referring again to Figure 1 for arrangement and number to make of each row.

Row 4	7 A, one each I, J and B
Row 6	11 A, one each J and B
Row 8	12 A, one each C and J
Row 10	22 A, one each K and G
Row 12	11 A, one each E, G and H

3. Join L1 and L2 strips together on short ends to make a Row 1; press seam to one side referring to Figure 2. Repeat to make eight of Row 1.

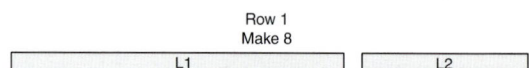

Figure 2

Tip

When joining long rows together, first pin mark the horizontal center of each row. Align and pin the strips right sides together at strip centers and ends. Pin raw edges together between centers and ends to help hold the layers together while stitching. This is one time a quilter should use pins when seaming.

Use an even-feed or walking foot when stitching long strips. This foot feeds both layers of fabric through the machine evenly.

Resist the temptation to pull the fabric layers through the machine. This will stretch the seam giving it a wavy appearance. Let your machine do the work and use your hands to guide the fabric.

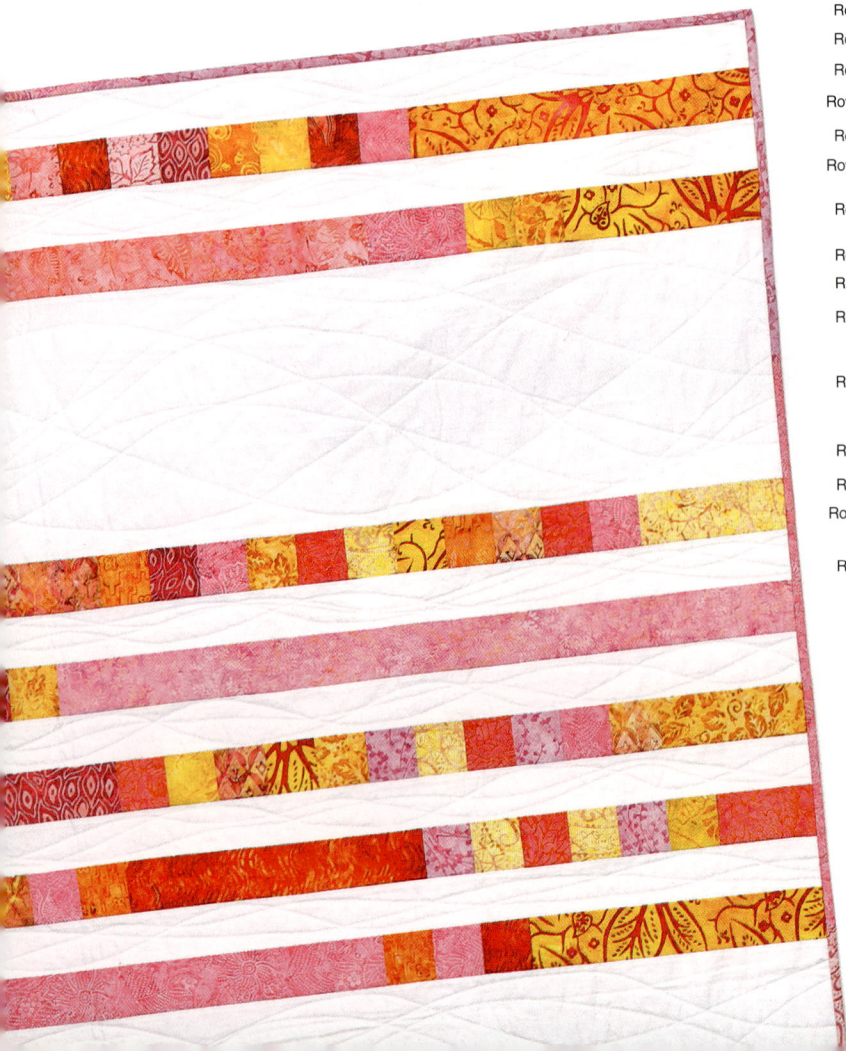

Completing the Quilt

1. Arrange the rows on a flat surface referring to the Assembly Diagram for correct order.

2. Join the rows in pairs along long edges beginning with Rows 1 and 2. Press seams open. **Note:** *You will have 11 pairs and one single row. Return rows to correct place in arrangement before stitching next pair.*

3. Join first two row pairs together; press seams open before adding another pair to the quilt. Repeat to join all rows and complete the quilt top.

4. Layer, quilt as desired and bind. ■

Row 1
Row 2
Row 1
Row 4
Row 3
Row 6
Row 1
Row 8
Row 1
Row 6
Row 1
Row 10
Row 1
Row 12
Row 5
Row 6
Row 1
Row 8
Row 7
Row 6
Row 1
Row 12
Row 9

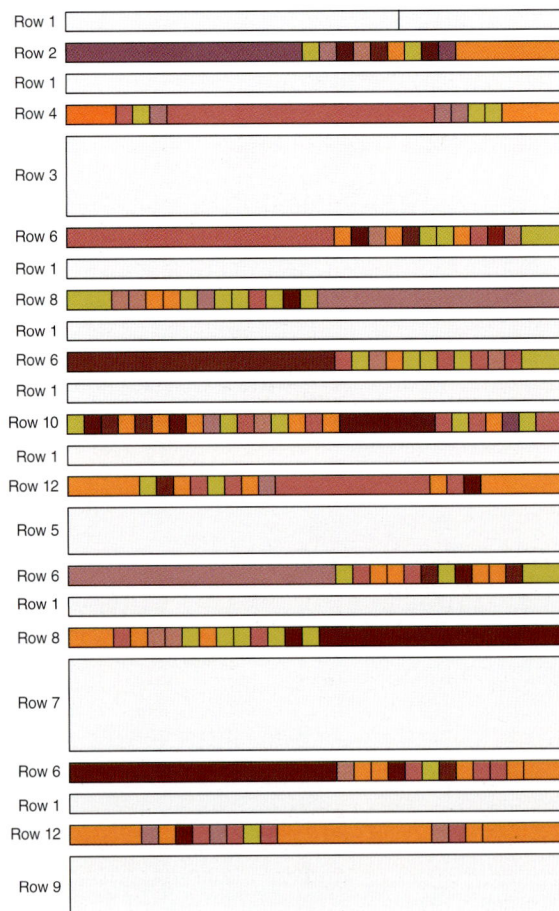

Pretty in Pink
Assembly Diagram 60" x 74"

Broken Crackers

Design by Carolyn S. Vagts for The Village Pattern Company

A precut package of 10" squares and a single afternoon
and you can have a quilt top completed.

Project Specifications

Skill Level: Beginner
Quilt Size: 40" x 64"
Block Size: 8" x 8"
Number of Blocks: 40

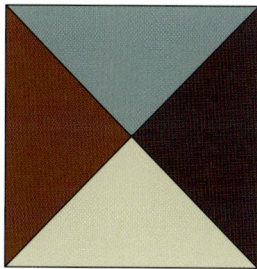

Broken Crackers
8" x 8" Block
Make 40

Materials

- 40 (10") precut squares
- ⅝ yard coordinating batik
- 3⅛ yards backing
- Batting 48" x 72"
- Thread
- Basic sewing tools and supplies

Cutting

1. Cut each 10" square in half on both diagonals to cut 160 quarter square triangles. *Note: You should be able to cut five squares at once with a sharp rotary cutter blade. Sort the squares into eight stacks of five squares each and cut.*

2. Cut six 2½" by fabric width strips coordinating batik for binding.

Completing the Blocks

1. Select two different quarter square triangles and stitch right sides together along one short side (Figure 1). Press seam to one side. Repeat to make 80 units.

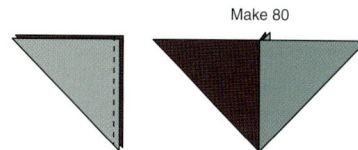

Make 80

Figure 1

2. Select two different units from step 1, match seams and stitch together referring to Figure 2. Press seams to one side. Repeat to make 40 Broken Crackers blocks referring to the block diagram.

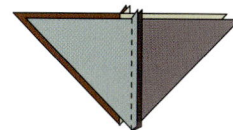

Figure 2

3. Trim the completed blocks to 8½" square. *Note: If using an 8½" square ruler, center the ruler over the block matching the diagonal line on the ruler to the block seams (Figure 3).*

Figure 3

Completing the Quilt

1. Lay out blocks on a flat surface in eight rows of five blocks each in a pleasing arrangement referring to the Assembly Diagram for suggestions.

2. Stitch blocks together in rows as arranged, returning each stitched row to the arrangement. Press seams in opposite directions row to row.

3. Stitch rows together as arranged and matching seams referring again to the Assembly Diagram. Press seams in one direction.

4. Layer, quilt as desired and bind. ■

Broken Crackers
Assembly Diagram 40" x 64"

Precuts to Yardage—Yardage to Precuts

You have precuts but the pattern you want to use lists yardage in the materials list. Or maybe you have yardage and the materials list is written for precuts. Just remember these equivalents.

One fat quarter (18" x 21") contains the same amount of usable fabric as ¼ yard (9" by fabric width).

One fat eighth (9" x 21") contains the same amount of usable fabric as ⅛ yard (4½" by fabric width).

Remember that 5" and 10" square and 2½" by fabric width bundles are all composed of a wide variety of complimentary fabrics. In order to have a similar variety when using yardage, you will need to divide the total yardage among several fabrics.

You can cut eight 5" squares from one 5" by fabric width strip. To figure yardage, divide the number of 5" squares required by 8, multiply by 5" and divide by 36". To figure how many 5" squares you can cut from a yardage amount, divide the yardage by 5" and multiply by 8.

You can cut four 10" squares from one 10" by fabric width strip. To figure yardage, divide the number of 10" squares required by 4, multiply by 10" and divide by 36". To figure how many 10" squares you can cut from a yardage amount, divide the yardage by 10" and multiply by 4.

You can cut one 2½" by fabric width strip from ⅛ yard. Decide how many different fabrics you will be using, multiply the number of strips you will be cutting from each fabric by 2½", and then round up to the nearest yardage amount. If you need 20 strips and have decided to use 20 different fabrics you will need ⅛ yard of each. If you decide that you only want to use five fabrics, you will need to cut four strips (a total of 10" by fabric width) from each fabric and will need at least ⅜ yard of each fabric.

If you have yardage and want to know how many 2½" by fabric width strips you can cut from that amount, divide the total yardage inches by 2½". To find the number of strips you can cut from ½ yard, divide 18" by 2½". You can cut seven strips from ½ yard.

Darts Bed Runner

Design by Julie Weaver

The geometric shape created using half-square triangles and the warm fabric choices make this perfect for any masculine bed.

Project Specifications

Skill Level: Confident Beginner
Quilt Size: 69" x 27"

Project Note

The designer chose to use the same brown and cream prints throughout this bed runner. Choose three different brown and cream prints and coordinating brown print yardage to give this bed runner a monochromatic scrappy look.

Materials

- 3 fat quarters brown prints
- 3 fat quarters cream prints
- ⅜ yard green print
- 1¾ yards coordinating brown print
- 2¼ yards backing
- Batting 77" x 35"
- Thread
- Basic sewing tools and supplies

Cutting

1. Cut a total of seven 4½" x 8½" C rectangles and 14 (4½") B squares from brown fat quarters.

2. Cut a total of seven 4½" x 8½" A rectangles and 14 (4½") D squares from brown fat quarters.

3. Cut six 1½" by fabric width E/F strips green print; subcut one strip into two 1½" x 16½" F strips. Set aside five strips.

4. Cut two 4½" by fabric width G strips coordinating brown print.

5. Cut five 6" by fabric width H/I strips coordinating brown print; subcut two strips into 6" x 27½" I side borders. Set aside four strips for H borders.

6. Cut five 2½" by fabric width strips coordinating brown print for binding.

Completing the Bed Runner Center

1. Draw a diagonal line from left to right on wrong side of each B and D square.

2. Position B on one corner of A and stitch together on drawn diagonal line as shown in Figure 1. Trim seam to ¼" and press B away from A. Stitch a B square on opposite corner of A, trimming and pressing as on previous corner. Repeat to make seven Light Flying Geese units.

Light Flying Geese Unit
Make 7

Figure 1

3. Repeat step 1 with C and D pieces to make seven Dark Flying Geese units (Figure 2).

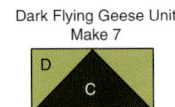

Dark Flying Geese Unit
Make 7

Figure 2

4. Select and join four Dark Flying Geese units and three Light Flying Geese units alternately as shown in Figure 3 to make Row 1.

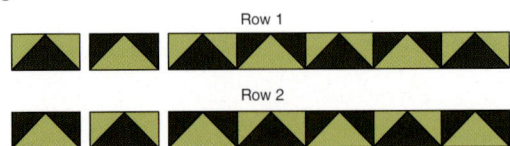

Row 1

Row 2

Figure 3

5. Select and join four Light Flying Geese units and three Dark Flying Geese units alternately referring again to Figure 3 to make Row 2.

6. Join five E/F strips together on short ends to make one long strip; press seams to one side. Cut four 1½" x 56½" E strips from long strip.

7. Join two E strips, Row 1, Row 2 and G along length as shown in Figure 4.

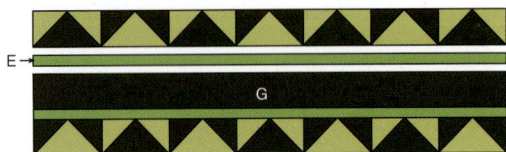

Figure 4

Completing the Bed Runner

1. Stitch F strips to both short ends of center unit; press seams toward F.

2. Join four H strips together on short ends to make one long strip; press seams to one side. Cut two 6" x 58½" H top and bottom borders.

3. Stitch H to top and bottom of bed runner; press seams toward H. Stitch I to both sides of bed runner; press seams toward I.

4. Layer, quilt as desired and bind. ▪

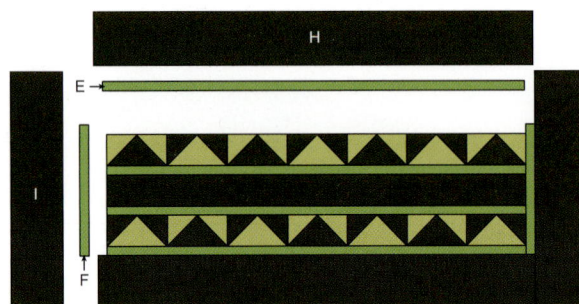

Darts Bed Runner
Assembly Diagram 69" x 27"

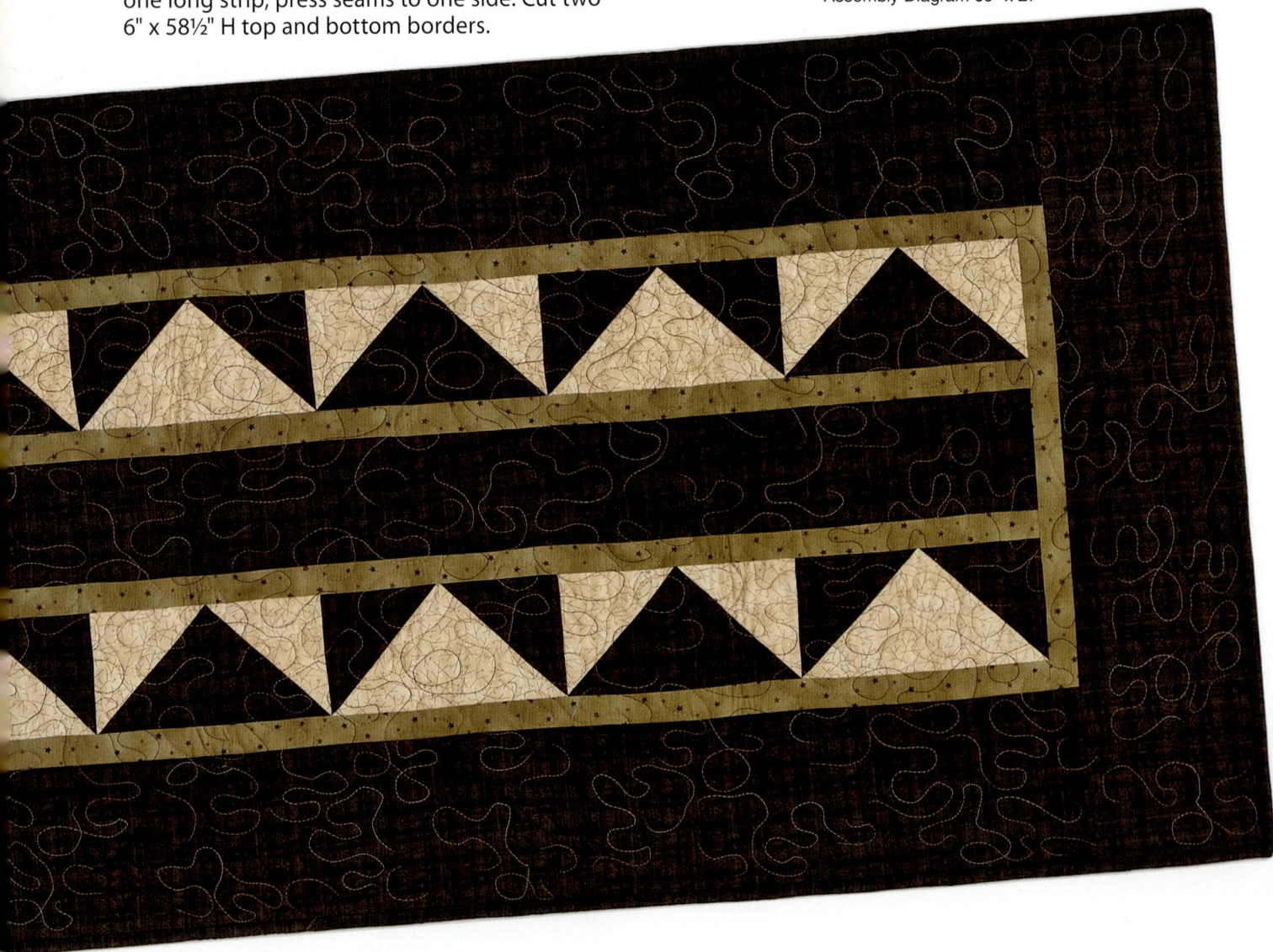

Bird's Eye View

Design by Gina Gempesaw

Quilted by Carole Whaling

Piece 2½" precut strips together to create brilliant sashing between simply charming piecing. This quilt would work with any fabric.

Project Specifications

Skill Level: Confident Beginner
Quilt Size: 72" x 89½"
Block Size: 10" x 10"
Number of Blocks: 32

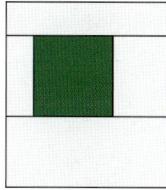

Bird's Eye View
10" x 10" Block
Make 32

Materials

- 32 (5") precut squares
- 40 (2½" by fabric width) precut strips
- 3⅞ yards white solid
- 5½ yards backing
- Batting 80" x 98"
- Thread
- Basic sewing tools and supplies

Cutting

1. Cut a total of 130 (2½" x 10") F rectangles and 10 (2½" x 5¼") G rectangles from the precut strips.

2. Cut five 5" by fabric width strips white solid; subcut strips into 32 each 4" x 5" A rectangles and 2" x 5" B rectangles.

3. Cut five 10" by fabric width strips white solid; subcut strips into 32 each 4" x 10" C rectangles and 2" x 10" D rectangles.

4. Cut two 5¼" by fabric width strips white solid; subcut eight 5¼" x 10" E rectangles.

5. Cut 16 (2½" by fabric width) strips white solid; set aside eight strips for H/I and eight strips for binding.

Completing the Blocks

1. Stitch a precut 5" square between B and A referring to Figure 1; press seams toward the precut square.

Figure 1

2. Stitch D to top and C to bottom of B-A-precut square unit and press seams toward C and D referring to Figure 2.

Figure 2

3. Repeat steps 1 and 2 to make 32 Bird's Eye blocks referring to the block diagram.

Completing the Quilt Center

1. Select and join eight assorted blocks and two E rectangles as shown in Figure 3 for block orientation. Repeat to make four block rows.

Make 4

Figure 3

2. Select and join nine F rectangles on short ends (Figure 4); press seams in one direction. Repeat to make 10 F strips.

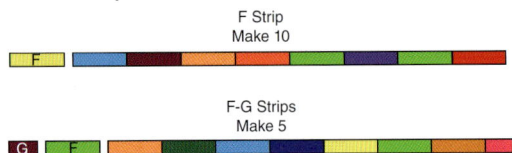

F Strip
Make 10

F-G Strips
Make 5

Figure 4

3. Select and join eight F rectangles and two G rectangles on short ends referring again to Figure 4; press seams in one direction. Repeat to make five F-G strips.

4. Stitch an F-G strip between two F strips referring to Figure 5; press seams toward F-G strips. Repeat to make five sashing units.

Sashing Unit
Make 5

Figure 5

5. Stitch the four block rows alternately with the five sashing units referring to the Assembly Diagram. Press seams away from the block rows.

Completing the Quilt

1. Join the H/I strips together on short ends to make one long strip; press seams in one direction.

2. Cut the long strip into two each 2½" x 85½" H and 2½" x 72½" I borders. Stitch H to both sides and I to top and bottom of quilt.

3. Layer, quilt as desired and bind. ■

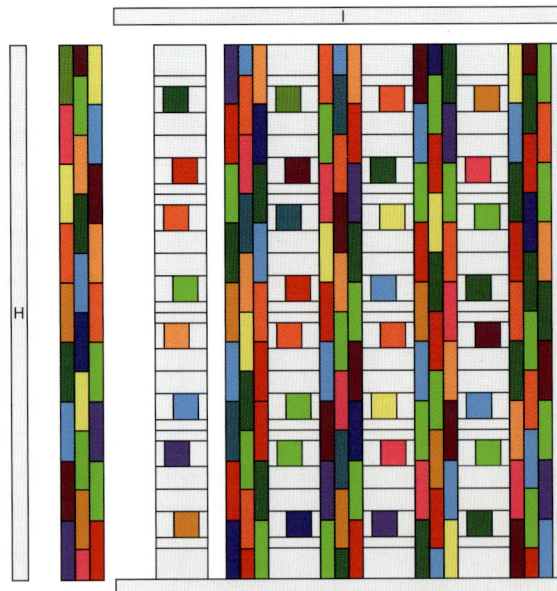

Bird's Eye View
Assembly Diagram 72" x 89¹/₂"

Dakota Bloomers

Design by Julie Weaver

This project is easy to make and uses up lots of fat eighths.
Piecing one of the borders is a really nice way to use the leftovers.

Project Specifications
Skill Level: Confident Beginner
Quilt Size: 57½" x 65"
Block Size: 9" x 9"
Number of Blocks: 16

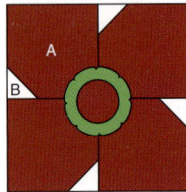

Dakota Bloomers
9" x 9" Block
Make 16

Materials
- 16 fat eighths bright floral print
- 2 fat eighths lime green print
- 1⅛ yards lime green solid
- 1½ yards white solid
- 4⅛ yards backing
- Batting 66" x 73"
- Thread
- 1 yard paper-backed fusible web
- Template material
- Basic sewing tools and supplies

Cutting
1. Prepare templates for Flower and Flower Center from patterns provided. Trace 16 Flowers and Flower Centers on paper side of paper-backed fusible web leaving ½" between shapes. Cut out shapes, leaving a margin around each.

2. Follow manufacturer's instructions to fuse 16 Flowers to wrong side of lime green print fat eighths. Cut out on traced lines. Do not remove paper backing.

3. Cut four 5" A squares from each bright floral print fat eighth.

4. Follow manufacturer's instructions to fuse one Flower Center to wrong side of each bright floral print fat eighth. Cut out on traced lines. Do not remove paper backing.

5. Cut a total of 44 (3" x 5½") J rectangles and four 3" K squares from the bright floral print fat eighths.

6. Cut six 1¼" by fabric width E strips lime green solid.

7. Cut five 1½" by fabric width F/G strips lime green solid.

8. Cut four 2" by fabric width strips white solid; subcut 64 (2") B squares.

9. Cut four 5" by fabric width strips white solid; subcut 16 (5" x 9½") C rectangles.

10. Cut 20 (1½" by fabric width) strips white solid. Set aside nine strips for D, five strips for H/I and six strips for L/M.

Completing the Blocks
1. Draw a diagonal line from left to right on each B square.

2. Select four like A squares and four B squares.

3. Position B on upper right corner of an A square. Stitch on line, trim seam to ¼" and press B away from A referring to Figure 1. Repeat with all four like A squares.

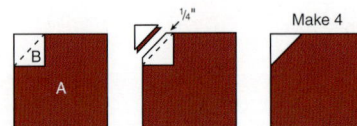

Figure 1

4. Arrange and join the A-B squares referring to the Dakota Bloomers block diagram for orientation.

5. Repeat steps 2–4 to make 16 A-B units.

6. Following manufacturer's instructions, fuse a Flower centered on an A-B unit referring to Figure 2.

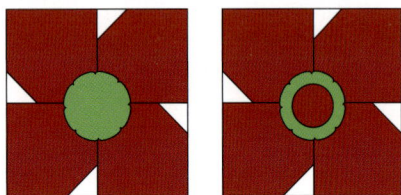

Figure 2

7. Center and fuse a Flower Center that matches the A squares in the A-B unit on the Flower referring again to Figure 2.

8. Machine blanket-stitch around the Flower and Flower Center edges to complete a Dakota Bloomers block (Figure 3).

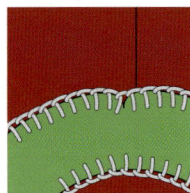

Figure 3

9. Repeat steps 6–8 to make 16 Dakota Bloomers blocks.

10. Select, arrange and join four blocks and four C rectangles into a row referring to Figure 4. Repeat to make four rows.

Row 1
Make 4

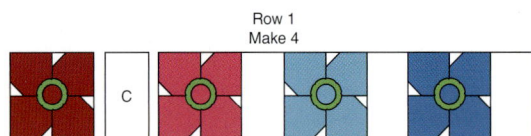

Figure 4

11. Stitch together D strips on short ends to make one long strip; press seams in one direction. Cut long strip into three 1½" x 54½" D sashing strips.

12. Stitch together E strips on short ends to make one long strip; press seams in one direction. Cut long strip into six 1¼" x 54½" E sashing strips.

13. Stitch a D sashing strip between two E sashing strips as shown in Figure 5; press seams toward D. Repeat to make three sashing rows.

Sashing Row
Make 3

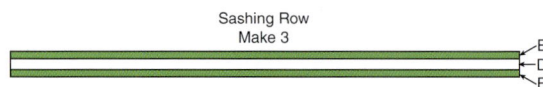

Figure 5

14. Stitch together four block rows and three sashing rows alternately, beginning with a block row and referring to the Assembly Diagram for block row orientation. Press seams away from block rows.

Completing the Quilt

1. Stitch together F/G strips on short ends to make one long strip; press seams in one direction. Cut long strip into two each 1½" x 54½" G and 1½" x 46½" F strips.

2. Stitch F to both sides and G to top and bottom of quilt center for first border, referring to the Assembly Diagram. Press seams toward F and G.

3. Stitch together H/I strips on short ends to make one long strip; press seams in one direction. Cut long strip into two each 1½" x 56½" H and 1½" x 48" I strips.

4. Stitch H to both sides and I to top and bottom of quilt center for second border, referring to the Assembly Diagram. Press seams toward H and I.

5. Join together two sets each of 12 and 10 J rectangles. Center and stitch one set of 12 J rectangles to each side of the quilt. Trim even with the quilt edges if necessary.

6. Trim 1½" from each end of both sets of 10 J rectangles. Join a K square to each end of each set referring to the Assembly Diagram. Stitch J-K sets to top and bottom of quilt to complete the third border referring again to the Assembly Diagram.

7. Stitch together L/M strips on short ends to make one long strip; press seams in one direction. Cut long strip into two each 1½" x 63½" L and 1½" x 55" M strips.

8. Stitch L to both sides and M to top and bottom of quilt center for fourth border, referring to the Assembly Diagram. Press seams toward L and M.

9. Layer, quilt as desired and bind. ◼

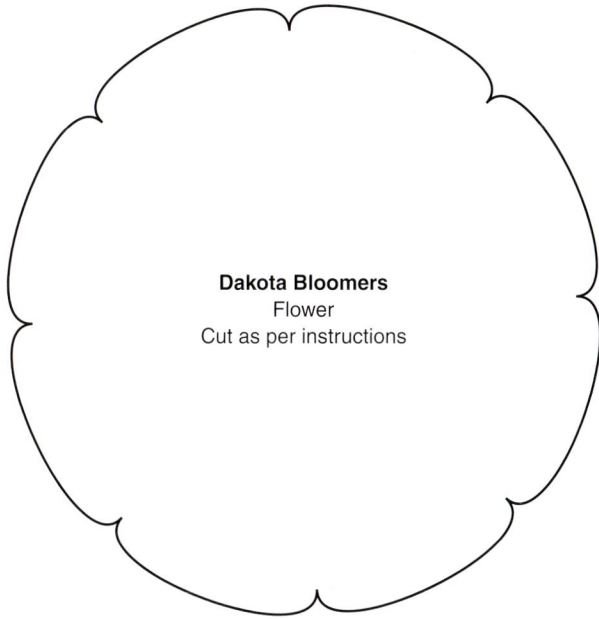

Dakota Bloomers
Flower
Cut as per instructions

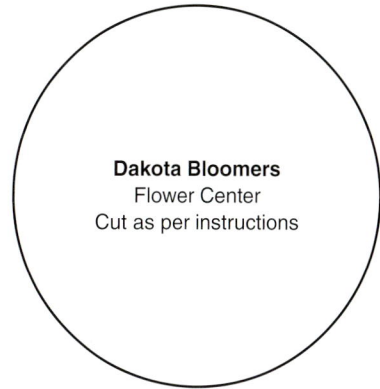

Dakota Bloomers
Flower Center
Cut as per instructions

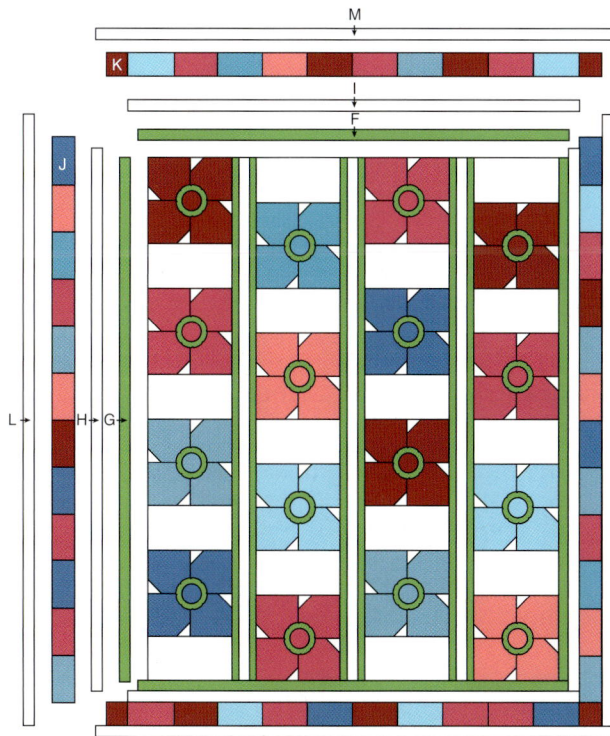

Dakota Bloomers
Assembly Diagram 57$\frac{1}{2}$" x 65"

Harvest Charm Runner

Design by Tricia Lynn Maloney

A collection of 5" squares will make this fast and
easy table runner. Make one for every season.

Project Specifications
Skill Level: Confident Beginner
Quilt Size: 57" x 19"

Materials
- 31 assorted 5" precut squares
- 2 yards backing
- Batting 23" x 61"
- Thread
- Bodkin (optional)
- Basic sewing tools and supplies

Completing the Table Runner Top

1. Arrange and stitch three 5" precut squares into a
row referring to Figure 1. Press seams in one direction. Repeat to make five A rows. *Note: Arrange the
precut squares so that all rows are different as seen in
the Assembly Diagram.*

A Row
Make 5

Figure 1

B Row
Make 4

Figure 2

2. Arrange and stitch four 5" precut squares into
a row referring to Figure 2. Press seams in one
direction. Repeat to make four B rows.

3. Select and join two A rows and one B row as
shown in Figure 3; press seams away from B row.
*Note: Arrange rows with seams pressed in opposite
directions to make matching seams easier. Repeat to
make two end units.*

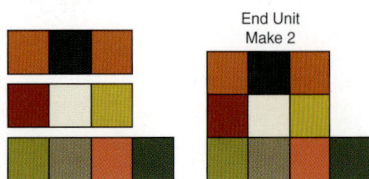

End Unit
Make 2

Figure 3

4. Select and join two B rows and one A row,
as shown in Figure 4, to make one center unit.
Note: Arrange rows with seams pressed in opposite
*directions to make matching seams easier. Press seams
toward A rows.*

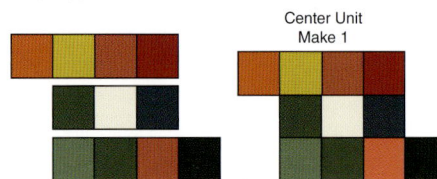

Center Unit
Make 1

Figure 4

5. Stitch an end unit to the center unit, matching
seams and referring to the Assembly Diagram.
Press seams in one direction.

Completing the Table Runner

1. Place the batting on a flat surface. Layer and
smooth the backing right side up on the batting.
Center and smooth the completed table runner top
right side down with the batting/backing layers. Pin
or baste layers together.

2. Stitch a ¼" seam around all edges, pivoting at
outside and inside corners. Leave an 8" opening for
turning on one end.

3. Trim batting and backing even with the table
runner top. Trim outside corners and clip inside
corners close to stitching.

4. Turn right side out. Carefully push out outside
corners and press edges flat. *Note: Use a bodkin or
other blunt object to push out corners.*

5. Press opening edges to inside; hand-stitch
opening closed. Quilt as desired. ■

Harvest Charm Runner
Assembly Diagram 57" x 19"

Celebrate America

Design by Lori Hein

Easy fusible appliqué, some solid fabrics and the use of
5" squares are all you need to make this fun miniature quilt.

Project Specifications
Skill Level: Intermediate
Quilt Size: 31½" x 27"

Materials
- 17 (5") precut squares tan solid
- 25 (5") precut squares cream solid
- ⅜ yard navy solid
- ½ yard red solid
- ½ yard gold solid
- 1⅛ yards backing
- Batting 40" x 36"
- Thread
- 2 yards paper-backed fusible web
- Template material
- Basic sewing tools and supplies

Cutting
1. Cut three 2½" by fabric width strips navy
for binding.

Preparing the Fusible Appliqué
1. Trace eight border star squares, three large stars
and four small stars on paper side and across the
width of the paper-backed fusible web. Leave
¼" between shapes.

2. Prepare a template of the wave shape provided.
Trace 3½ wave shapes, end to end, on the paper side
and along the length of the paper-backed fusible
web. Repeat to trace four 35"-long wave shapes.

3. Trace four swirl shapes on paper side and along
length of paper-backed fusible web, leaving
¼" between shapes.

4. Cut out all shapes, leaving a margin around
outside edges.

5. Follow manufacturer's instructions and fuse
border star squares, two large stars and one small
star to wrong side of navy solid. Cut out center star
from border star squares. Do not remove paper.

6. Fuse waves and one each small and large star to
wrong side of red solid and swirls and two small
stars to wrong side of gold solid. Cut out shapes;
do not remove paper.

Completing the Quilt
1. Select, arrange and join four tan and three cream
5" squares alternately beginning with a tan square
to make a top border.

2. Repeat step 1 with three tan and four cream
5" squares beginning with a cream square to make
a bottom border.

3. Follow manufacturer's instructions and fuse two
red solid waves centered on the top and bottom
borders referring to Figure 1. Trim waves even with
borders. Machine buttonhole-stitch wave edges
with matching thread.

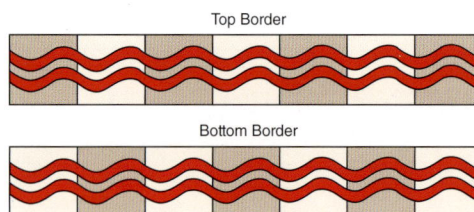

Top Border

Bottom Border

Figure 1

4. Center and fuse a border star square on a cream
5" square (Figure 2). Machine buttonhole-stitch
border star square and star cutout edges with
matching thread. Repeat to appliqué eight
cream squares.

Figure 2

5. Join four border star appliquéd squares together to make a side border. Repeat to make a second side border.

6. Join four each tan and cream 5" squares together to make four units of one each tan and cream square.

7. Referring to Figure 3, appliqué swirls on 5" square units. Position swirl curves on tan squares on two units and on cream squares on two units. Finish swirl edges with machine buttonhole-stitch with matching thread.

Figure 3

8. Center and appliqué two navy large stars and one each red solid and gold solid small stars on tan 5" squares referring to Figure 4 for positioning.

Figure 4

9. Position and appliqué a red solid large star and gold solid small star on cream 5" squares referring again to Figure 4.

10. Position and appliqué a navy small star on a swirl unit referring to Figure 5.

Figure 5

11. Arrange and join the swirl units, appliquéd squares, two tan and three cream 5" squares as shown in Assembly Diagram into four rows. Stitch rows together referring again to Assembly Diagram.

12. Stitch a star side border to each side of the quilt.

13. Stitch wave top border to top and wave bottom border to bottom of quilt.

14. Layer, quilt as desired and bind. ■

Celebrate America
Assembly Diagram 31½" x 27"

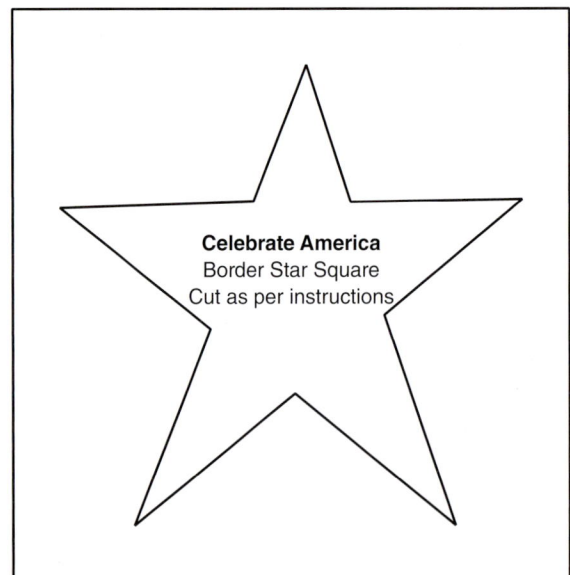

Celebrate America
Border Star Square
Cut as per instructions

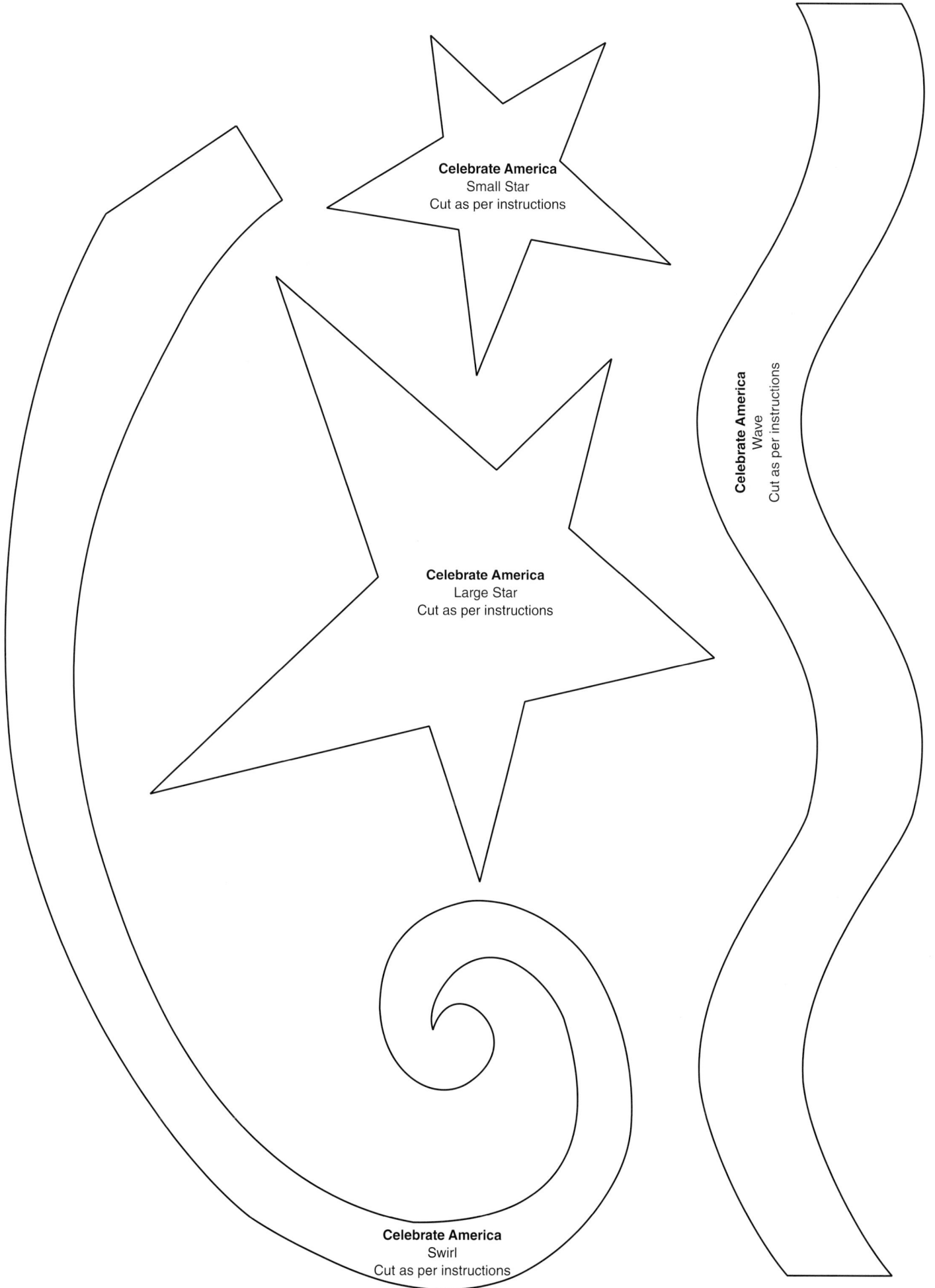

Celebrate America
Small Star
Cut as per instructions

Celebrate America
Large Star
Cut as per instructions

Celebrate America
Wave
Cut as per instructions

Celebrate America
Swirl
Cut as per instructions

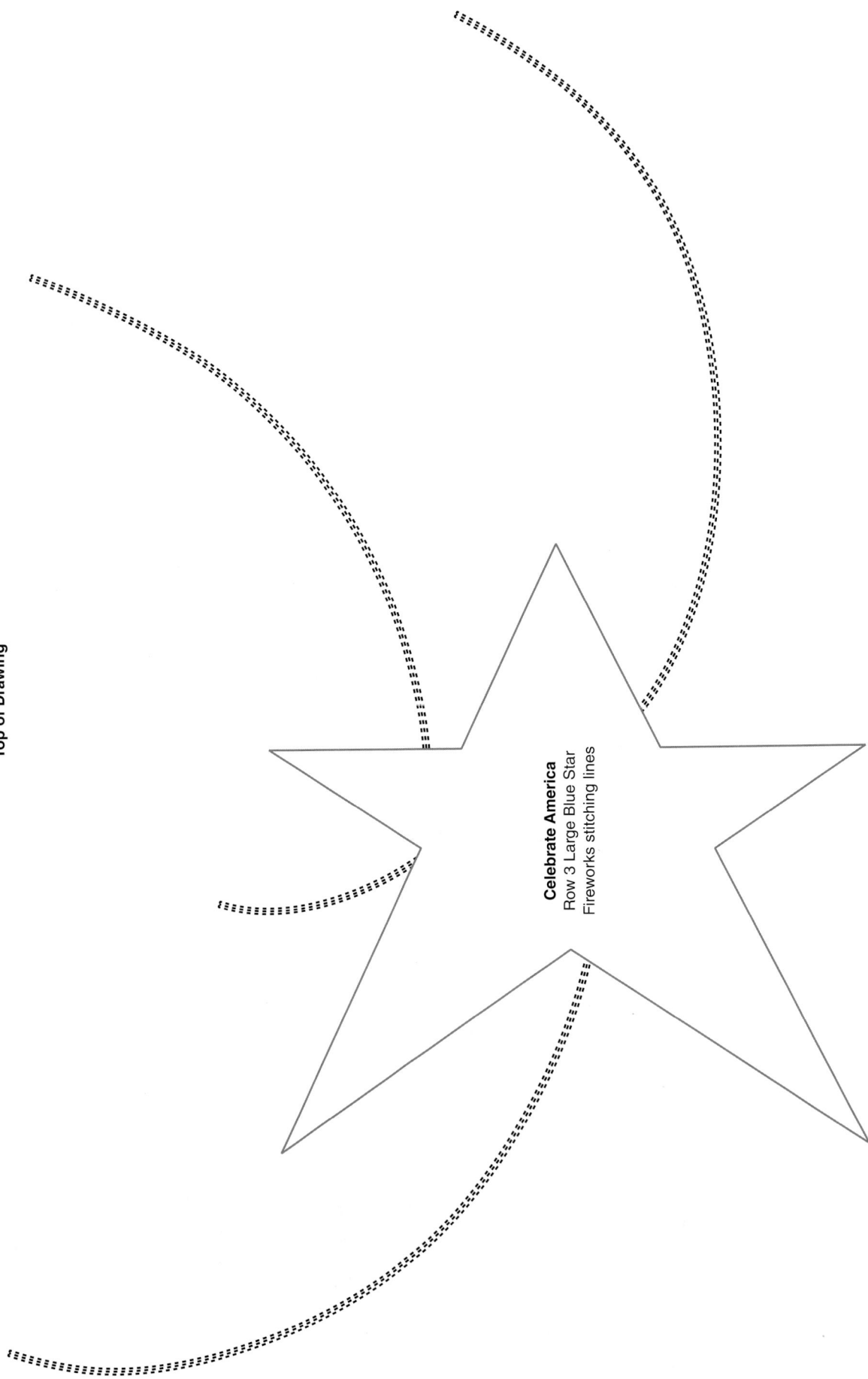

Celebrate America
Row 3 Large Blue Star
Fireworks stitching lines

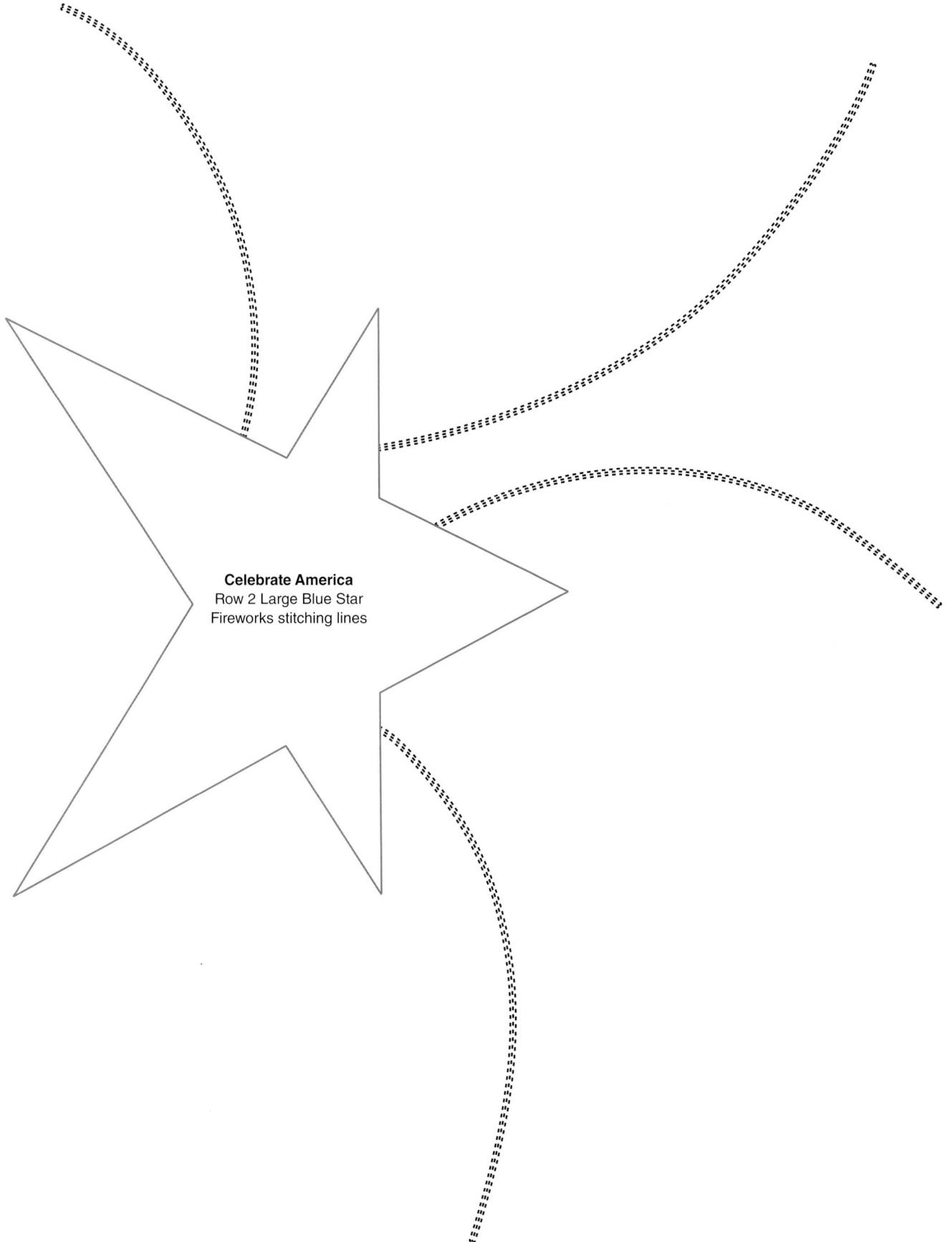

Celebrate America
Row 2 Large Blue Star
Fireworks stitching lines

Special Thanks

We would like to thank these individuals and/or manufacturers for their generosity.

Macaron Star, page 4: Bali Pops (2½" by fabric width) and fat quarter batiks from Hoffman Fabrics.

Apple of My Eye, page 9: Apple of My Eye collection fat quarters from Riley Blake Designs; Tuscany Silk batting by Hobbs; Aurifil Mako 50 weight cotton thread.

Warm Eyes, page 13: Tapestry by Fig Tree & Co. fat quarters for Moda.

Summer Twist, page 16: Juggling Summer Charm packs (5" squares) by Zen Chic and Bella Solids from Moda.

Hanging Lanterns, page 19: Izumi screen print collection fat eighths from Hoffman Fabrics; Soft & Toasty™ cotton batting from Fairfield; Superior Highlights gold from Superior Threads.

Pretty in Pink, page 24: Tonga Pink Lemonade Treats Strips (2½" by fabric width) and Soho Solids from Timeless Treasures.

Darts Bed Runner, page 30: A Year to Crow About collection fat quarters by Jacqueline Paton for Red Rooster Fabrics; Warm & Natural® batting from The Warm Company.

Bird's Eye View, page 33: Tonga Gumdrop batik Treats Strips (2½" by fabric width) and Minis (5" squares) from Timeless Treasures.

Dakota Bloomers, page 36: Gypsy Girl collection by Lily Ashbury and Bella Solids fat eighths from Moda; Lite Steam-A-Seam 2® fusible web from The Warm Company; Thermore® batting from Hobbs.

Celebrate America, page 42: Bella Solids Neutral Charm packs (5" squares) and yardage from Moda.

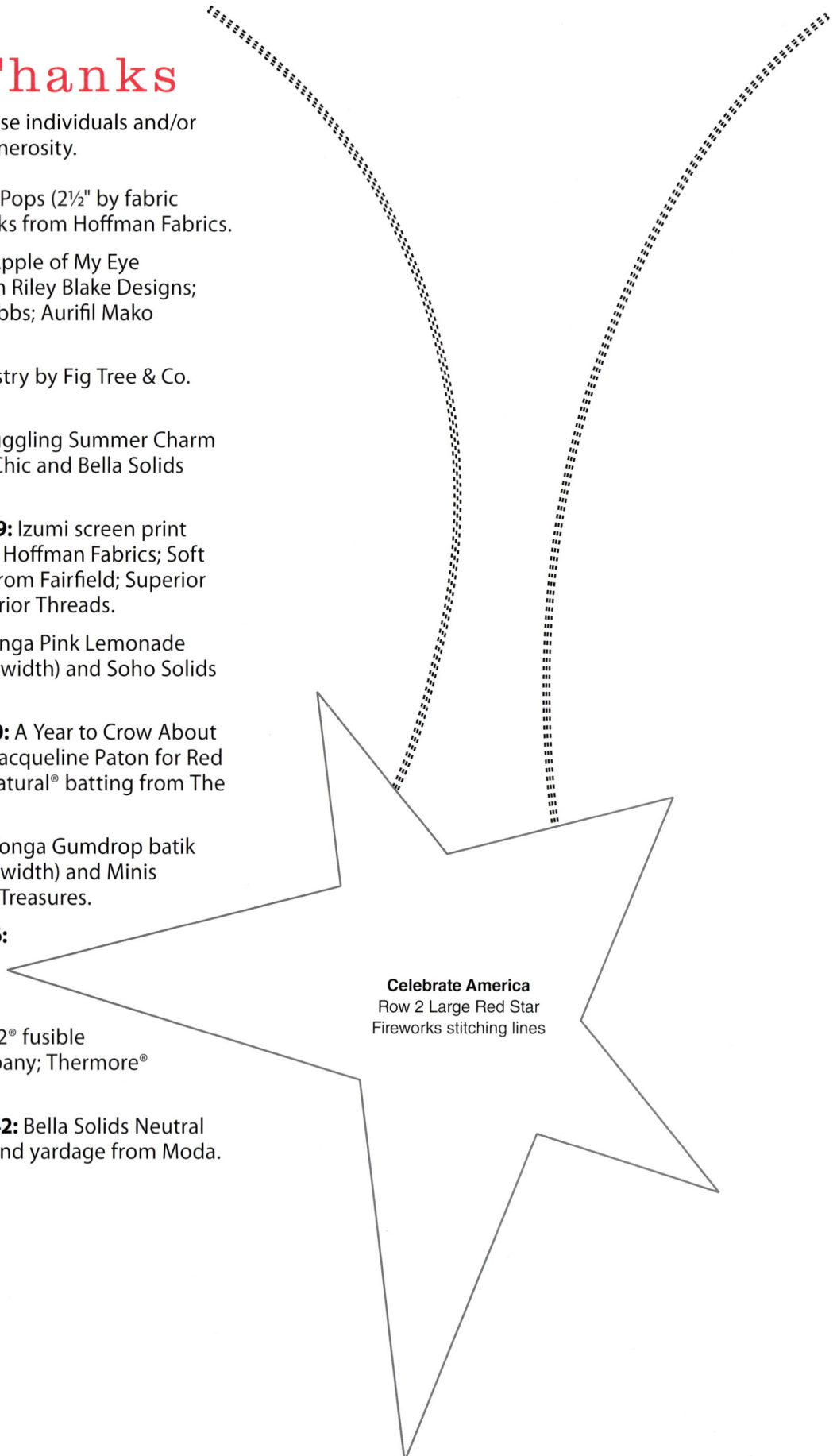

Celebrate America
Row 2 Large Red Star
Fireworks stitching lines